The Ashtavakra Gita... - Primary Source Edition

Baij Nath (Lala.)

with the truest labours
the pfregards — JUL 1? 1907

JUL 15 1907

THE
Ashtavakra Gita

being a dialogue between King Janaka and Rishi
Ashtavakra on Vedanta

PUBLISHED WITH

Sanskrit Text and English Translation and
Introduction

BY

RAI BAHADUR LALA BAIJ NATH, B. A.,

FELLOW OF THE ALLAHABAD UNIVERSITY,

Officiating District and Sessions Judge, Benares

AND

*Author of Hinduism ; Ancient and Modern ; England and
India ; Plague in India ; India Past and Present,
(Urdu) Shashtroktupasna (Hindi) &c. &c.*

NEW EDITION,
Revised and Enlarged.

1907.

Published at the Office of the Vaishya Hit-
kari, Meerut.

1,000 COPIES.

PRINTED AT THE NEWUL KISHORE PRESS, ALLAHABAD.

TO THE

LATE SWAMI RAMA TIRTHAJI MAHARAJA, M. A.,

THIS LITTLE BOOK IS

DEDICATED AS

A TOKEN OF LOVE

BY ONE OF HIS

Sorrowing friends and

ADMIRERS

The Translator.

CONTENTS.

IndL 3241, 2.10

ERRATA.

INTRODUCTION.

Page	Line	For	Read
1	21	ones	one's
3	24	itself	himself
10	16	eigth	eighth
15	5	absve	above

TEXT.

Page	Line	For	Read
2	11	मानसनि	मानसानि
12	1	चित्तवाते	चित्तवाते .
19	2	realisation	realization
21	4	concernedness	unconcernedness
"	(note) 10	pray's	pries
41	13	a rare	rare
46	(note) 8	connect	connects
47	2	allowment	attainment
69	(note) 8	loss	lost
70	9	शुपुसिवा	शुषुसिर्वा
"	15	क्ष	क्ष
74	(note) 24	cansality	causality

INTRODUCTION.

THE aim of all true philosophy is to raise man from the finite to the infinite and to make him indifferent to the world of sense around him. This has also been the goal of all true religion, and more so in India than elsewhere. Here from time immemorial this solid seeming world has been looked upon as a dream, God as the only reality and the merging of the individual into the Universal Self as the highest aim of life. Intellect however highly cultivated, duty however well performed, was never thought here to lead man to that which is beyond the intellect. Both left him many a stage lower and it was only through complete renunciation, entire forgetfulnes of self, that he could realize the Self—the Átmá within as the Self of all, and secure freedom from the ever-recurring round of the Sansára and therefore bliss everlasting. "There is no hope of immortality from wealth." "Where the I is, the Infinite is not. When the I ceases to be I, the Infinite shines in all its glory." "The knower of Self (Átmá) only crosses the ocean of sorrow." "Where there is duality there is fear." When all has become one's ownself, what is there to be afraid of. Unity alone is fearlessness. These are the dicta of philosophers and sages of India on the subject of religion and philosophy.

Various steps have been indicated for the attainment of this ideal, but they are all summed up in the words, *renunciation of desire and destruction of all sense of duality.* The Yogváshishtha, one of the most respected authorities on the subject, describes them as the seven stages of Yoga or Gyána, union with or knowledge of the Supreme. The first is right desire (*subhechá*).

When man after having tasted the pleasures of the senses, finds them all to be unreal and resulting in nothing but pain, and turns his thoughts inwards, he begins to question himself as to what after all is this panorama known as the world, what have I to do in it, how far actions which give but fleeting fruits can serve my highest end, why should I waste my life in taking part in this juggler's show, what should I do to cross this ocean of life, where shall I find bliss which knows of no decay ? Actuated by this desire he avoids all foolish or idle talk, does not take pleasure in the frivolities of ordinary life, loves solitude and avoids society, does all the good he can, shuns evil, and does nothing which is likely to cause pain to others. His words become full of sweetness and wisdom and he begins to have love for all. Even this tends to raise him higher than his fellows and brings the god in him into greater prominence. But he does not stop here. On the contrary wherever and whenever he can, he seeks the company of the wise and the good and devotes his time to the study of, and meditation upon, the problems of life. Firmly resolved to cross the ocean of the world, he lives constantly in the company of those who both by learning and practice of Truth are likely to lead him onwards. Performance of good actions and controlling of the mind and senses from running astray, become a part of his nature and he enters the second stage known as the *Suvicharná* or right meditation. Here he sees what he has to do, what not, distinguishes between the spheres of knowledge and ignorance, learns form his teacher and the Sastras, what he is, what is the world around him and what is God ; and tries to subdue the little of pride, passion, avarice or attachment to the things of the world that may have yet been left in him.

He is now ready for the third stage known as the *asan-sangini*—(non-attachment) where he cuts himself off from society more completely, betakes himself to solitude and passes his time in contemplation, on the banks of sacred rivers, in jungles or in the hills. Study of sacred scriptures, reflection upon their meaning, constant thought of the vanities of the world, performance of religious duties occupy his time and prepare him for further development. Two kinds of non-attachment (Vairágya) now dawn upon him. The first is where he sees himself neither as the doer of action nor the enjoyer of the fruit thereof nor standing in the way of another doing what pleases him. He no longer attaches himself to anything whatever, but knows that God ordains all and that happiness or misery is not of his doing. Realizing that all activity of the *manas* (concrete mind) leads, to nothing but misery, he lets it have as little work as possible, and prepares himself for fuller renunciation of things of the world. Company of the good, study and reflection constantly practised, soon lead him on to the second stage of non-attachment where he finds that for him there is nothing left to do but to abide in his own self. His mind does not now run towards things of the outside world, but self-centred seeks to merge itself into that which is Truth, Infinity and Bliss itself. This in Yoga philosophy is described under the heads of *Yama* and *Niyama*. The former comprises abstention from (1) causing injury to others, (2) untruth, (3) incontenence, (4) theft, and (5) greed, and the latter observance of (1) purity, (2) contentment (3) self-control, study and resignation to the will of God. If one who has attained to this stage dies before he has reached the final stages of knowledge, he incarnates in the family of the good, the wise, and the pious, where the practices of his former life serve to carry him onwards. In these three stages which interlap each other, the world does not quite cease to exist though it loses the reality it once possessed. They are therefore called the waking states (*jágrat*). Persons who have attained to these three stages, act their part in life but in a spirit of greater tranquillity than others. Such men serve as beacon lights to humanity. Good becomes a part of their nature and evil can never come out of them. What they do, they do for others and their actions are guided by that highest of motives, the absence of self. Divine men like Rama, Janaka, Bhishma, Krishna and Yudhishthira, among house-holders, and Vashishtha, Viswamitra, Vyasa and Sankara may be cited as examples of those who acted their respective part in life, either as teachers of mankind, or as kings ruling their kingdoms for the good of their subjects, or as counsellors of kings, or as generals fighting for their cause, or as authors of works which live as long as the world lasts. The next four stages are the stages of Dharna (concentration) Dhyána (meditation) and Samádhi (absorption) of the Yoga Sastra. The fourth stage of Gyána (*Satwápatti*), is that of the accession of purity where the world appears like a dream. It has now lost its character of existence separate from the Infinite and is cognized as Truth and Bliss itself. But though Unity is here cognized, the duality is not yet fully merged into it. The mind, however, now rests in pure goodness (Sudhasatva), though the other two attributes of Rajas and Tamas have not yet altogether ceased to exist. In the next stage, the stage of complete nonattachment (*asansakti*), the mind becomes entirely detached from the visible like one in deep and peaceful slumber. It does not function, though it exists in latency. All duality has disappeared, all specific cognition gone, and the sage abides more completely in the Infinite. His actions now become like those of a child, simple and guileless, and yet he carries on the ordinary functions of life. His thought is however constantly directed towards his Átmá. In ancient Hindu literature men like Suka and Bharata attained to this condition. In modern times such instances are rather rare. The next stage is *Turyá*, the fourth condition, which transcends the states of wakefulness, dream and deep slumber. For one who abides in it, nothing appears to exist but Brahman, the Truth, the Infinite. For him there is neither existence nor non-existence, neither the I nor the absence thereof. Meditation of non-duality and avoidance of duality have ceased to be necessary for him. All doubt has disappeared. All fetters of the heart have been cut asunder. If the Karma which has given him his present incarnation, is yet unexhausted, he lives it out, but he is no longer of the world nor of anything in it. He is a *jiwan mukta* or one emancipated in life. Like a lamp in a windless spot, supremely blessed, full in and out, as if he had gained something unusual, but in reality abiding in that which was in him always, the Brahman, he becomes verily Brahman himself. The last stage is that which is beyond the fourth—*Turyátita*. It is not an object of speech or thought. Some call it Brahman, some Siva, some the supreme abode of Vishnu, some the separation of the Prakriti (nature) from the Purusha (the Supreme Self). All these are, however, names serving to convey but an imperfect notion of that of which no notion can be conveyed by anything in human language or anything appertaining to human thought. On entering this stage the sage becomes a *videhmukta* or free from embodied existence. Like rivers losing their name and form in the wide ocean, the sage free from both name and form attains to that which is beyond all, the Supreme, the Ever-effulgent Purusha. Knowing Brahman he becomes Brahman itself.

This is the goal of the philosophy of India which has led its wisest and best out of the Sansara. It still exercises and shall always exercise a deep influence over the lives and thoughts of all its people. The conditions of modern life are generally not so favourable to its attainment as those in which life was simpler. But even now men and women of all ranks and conditions look upon it as the crowning work of life. It has a fascination for them which outsiders can but faintly appreciate. The highest and the best here seek no other happiness but to avoid this recurring cycle of birth and re-birth which to them is fraught with nothing but misery. Kings sacrifice for it their thrones. The rich relinquish for it their most valued possessions, and men of education and position all their prospects in life and cutting all ties asunder betake themselvse to a life of mendicancy.

Most notable instances of this are daily seen in even India of to-day. Up in the Himalayas and elsewhere also will be found men possessed of the highest culture and the most refined ideas, devoting their lives to study and realization of the great problems of existence. With the fewest personal wants, with no thought of self, with the most frugal fare and a small hut to take shelter in, they possess a peace of mind and serenity of temper, the surest indices of the peace within. One has only to sit at the feet

स शरीरमहो विश्वं परित्यज्य मयाऽधुना ॥
कुतश्चित्कौशलादेव परमात्मा विलोक्यते ॥ ३ ॥

3. Having renounced this world together with the
body, I now somehow perceive the Supreme Self
through wisdom acquired by the teaching of the
Master.

यथा न तोयतो भिन्नास्तरंगाः फेनबुद्बुदाः ॥
आत्मनो न तथा भिन्नं विश्वमात्मविनिर्गतम् ॥४॥

4. Just as waves, foam and bubbles are not other
than the water from which they emanate, even so is
the world which has emanated from the Atma, no
other than the Atma.

तंतुमात्रो भवेदेव पटो यद्वद्विचारितः ॥
आत्मतन्मात्रमेवेदं तद्विश्वं विचारितम् ॥ ५ ॥

5. Just as cloth, when considered in its true nature,
is nothing but threads, even so is the world, duly considered, nothing but the Atma.

यथैवेक्षुरसे क्लृप्ता तेन व्याप्तैव शर्करा ॥
तथा विश्वं मयि क्लृप्तं मया व्याप्तं निरंतरम् ॥६॥

mine. Whose is this wealth ! No one's. Knowing this, I see nothing
that is mine. Taking my stand upon this, I have relinquished all sense
of mine. Listen now to that conviction by which I find every thing to
be mine. Not for my own sake do I seek objects of smell, taste, sight,
touch or hearing, even though they come in contact with my nose, tongue,
eyes, hand and ears. Thus have I conquered the earth, water, fire, air and
space of which they are the attributes. Not for my own sake do I seek
the mind in me though it be, thus have I conquered the mind. All these
do I seek for the service of the deities, the forefathers, the guests and all
beings. Thus everything is mine."—Mahabharta, Aswamedha Parva, Chap. 32.

6. Just as sugar pervades the juice of the sugar-cane, and sweetness pervades sugar, even so is the world imposed upon Me and I pervade the world [1].

आत्माज्ञानाज्जगद्भाति आत्मज्ञानान्न भासते ॥
रज्वज्ञानादहिर्भाति तज्ज्ञानान्नासते न हि ॥ ७ ॥

7. The world appears to exist from ignorance of the Self. With the knowledge of Self it ceases to exist. The snake appears to exist from ignorance of the rope, with the perception of the rope as such, the snake ceases to exist.

प्रकाशो मे निजं रूपं नातिरिक्तोऽस्म्यहं ततः ॥
यदा प्रकाशते विश्वं तदाहंभास एव हि ॥ ८ ॥

8. Light is my inmost nature. No other than Light am I. When the world is illumined, it is I that illumine it.

अहो विकल्पितं विश्वमज्ञानान्मयि भासते ॥
रूप्यं शुक्तौ फणी रज्जौ वारि सूर्यकरे यथा ॥ ९ ॥

9. Oh ! The world superimposed upon me exists in me through ignorance, like silver in the mother of pearl, the snake in the rope and the water of the mirage in the sunlight.

मत्तो विनिर्गतं विश्वं मय्येव लयमेष्यति ॥
मृदि कुंभो जले वीचिः कनके कटकं यथा ॥ १० ॥

10. The world which has emanated from me resolves itself in me, as the pot in the clay, the wave in

---

(1) i. e., The world which is pervaded by Me of the nature of bliss is nothing but Bliss (Ananda) itself.

the ocean and the armlet in the gold of which it is composed.

अहो अहं नमो महां विनाशो यस्य नास्ति मे ॥
ब्रह्मादिस्तंबपर्यंतं जगन्नाशेऽपि तिष्ठतः ॥ ११ ॥

11. Oh, Wonderful am I ! Reverence to My own Self which knows of no decay and which survives even the destruction of the whole world, from Brahmá to a blade of grass.

अहो अहं नमो महामेकोऽहं देहवानपि ॥
क्वचिन्न गंता नागंता व्याप्य विश्वमवस्थितः ॥१२॥

12. Oh, wonderful am I ! I bow to my own Self which, though associated with various bodies, is one, never coming nor going anywhere but pervading all.

अहो अहं नमो महां दक्षो नास्तीह मत्समः ॥
असंस्पृश्य शरीरेण येन विश्वं चिरं धृतम् ॥१३॥

13. Wonderful am I, Reverence to my own Self. None is wiser than I, who though untouched with the body, yet carry the world in Me for ever.

अहो अहं नमो महां यस्य मे नास्ति किंचन ॥
अथवा यस्य मे सर्वं यद्वाङ्मनसगोचरम् ॥ १४ ॥

14. Oh, wonderful am I ! Salutation to my own Self, to whom nothing here belongs, or yet to whom belongs all that is within the range of speech and thought.

ज्ञानं ज्ञेयं तथा ज्ञाता त्रितयं नास्ति वास्तवम् ॥
अज्ञानाद्भाति यत्रेदं सोऽहमस्मि निरंजनः ॥१५॥

15. Knowledge, knower and the object of knowledge do not in truth exist. That in which from ignorance, these three appear to exist, That am I, the spotless.

हेतमूलमहो दुःखं नान्यत्तस्यास्ति भेषजम् ॥
दृदयमेतन्मृषा सर्वं एकोहं चिद्रसोऽमलः ॥ १६ ॥

16. Oh ! Sorrow has its root in duality. There is no other cure for it except realization of the unreality of the visible and that I am the One Bliss, Intelligence, and Purity.

बोधमात्रोऽहमज्ञानादुपाधिः कल्पितो मया ॥
एवं विमृशतो नित्यं निर्विकल्पे स्थितिर्मम ॥१७॥

17. Knowledge alone am I ; I have imposed limitation upon my own Self from ignorance. Constantly reflecting upon this I have now found rest in That which is beyond the mind.

न मे बंधोऽस्ति मोक्षो वा भ्रांतिः शांता निराश्रया ॥
अहो मयि स्थितं विश्वं वस्तुतो न मयि स्थितम् ॥१८॥

18. Release or bondage is not mine. All this ceaseless illusion has gone. Oh ! the world is in me, or in truth is not in me.[1]

सशरीरमिदं विश्वं न किंचिदिति निश्चितम् ॥
शुद्धचिन्मात्र आत्मा च तत्कस्मिन्कल्पनाधुना ॥१९॥

(1) The aim of the Vedanta is not the establishment of non-duality, but the removal of duality due to error. The Atma or self which is the knower himself can not be the object of knowledge, or as said in the Upanishad-"how can one know that by which he knows all this ; by what can he know the knower ?"

19. This world with the body is nothing, this I have ascertained. The Atmá is Pure Intelligence itself, how can then there be any superimposition of the one upon the other ?

शरीरं स्वर्गनरकौ बंधमोक्षौ भयं तथा ॥

कल्पनामात्रमेवैतार्कि मे कार्यं चिदात्मनः ॥२०॥

20. The body, heaven and hell, release, bondage and fear, all these are mere imagination. What is there for Me whose nature is *Chit* [1] to do ?

अहो जनसमूहेऽपि न द्वैतं पश्यतो मम ॥

अरण्यमिव संवृतं क रतिं करवाण्यहम् ॥ २१ ॥

21. Oh ! for Me who see no duality even in the midst of a crowd, there is a forest even here, what shall I attach myself to ?

नाहं देहो न मे देहो जीवो नाहमरं हि चित् ॥

अयमेव हि मे बंध आसीद्या जीविते स्पृहा ॥२२॥

22. I am not this body, nor is the body mine. I am not the Jiva (individualized self), I am the *Chit*. This was indeed my bondage that I was attached to embodied existence. [2]

अहो भुवनकल्लोलैर्विचित्रैर्द्राक् समुत्थितम् ॥

मय्यनंतमहांभोधौ चित्तवाते समुद्यते ॥ २३ ॥

23. Oh ! in me, the limitless ocean, on the rising of the wind of the mind. arise waves in the shape of innumerable worlds of diverse description.

---

(1) "For the Yogi who has drunk deep of the nectar of wisdom, there is nothing left to do. If there is, he is not a knower of self." This is the declaration of Vedanta. Heaven, hell, sastras and their injunctions are all for the man of the world who believes the illusory to be real, not for the sage who has arisen above the world.

(2) This desire of life is one of the five off-shoots of Avidya and shall have to be killed before the knowledge of Self is gained.

मय्यनंतमहांभोधौ चित्तवाते प्रशाम्यति ॥
अभाग्याज्जीववणिजो जगत्पोतो विनश्वरः ॥२४॥

24. With the cessation of the wind of the mind, the boat of the unfortunate trader, the embodied self, disappears in Me, the great fathomless Ocean.

मय्यनंतमहांभोधावाश्चर्यं जीववीचयः ॥
उद्यंति घ्नंति खेलंति प्रविशंति स्वभावतः ॥२५॥

25. In Me, the great fathomless Ocean, waves of diverse individualized selves arise, strike each other, play and disappear in a wonderful manner.

CHAPTER 3.

Test of the Disciple's Self-realization.

अविनाशिनमात्मानमेकं विज्ञाय तत्त्वतः ॥
तवात्मज्ञस्य धीरस्य कथमर्थार्जने रतिः ॥ १ ॥

1. Says the master.—Knowing the Atma to be *the* One indestructible Self, how art thou, a sage, a knower of the Self, still attached to the acquisition of wealth ?

आत्माज्ञानादहो प्रीतिर्विषयभ्रमगोचरे ॥
शुक्तेरज्ञानतो लोभो यथा रजतविभ्रमे ॥ २ ॥

2. My pupil ! affection for objects which are in their nature illusory, arises from ignorance of the Self, just as desire, for a piece of mother of pearl mistaken for silver, arises from ignorance of the mother of pearl.

विश्वं स्फुरति यत्रेदं तरंगा इव सागरे ॥
सोऽहमस्मीति विज्ञाय किं दीन इव धावसि ॥३॥

3. Having known thyself to be that in which this world appears to exist like waves in the ocean, why dost thou run about like one who is helpless !

श्रुत्वापि शुद्धचैतन्यमात्मानमतिसुंदरम् ॥
उपस्थेऽत्यंतसंसक्तो मालिन्यमधिगच्छति ॥ ४ ॥

4. Having heard of the Self which is Pure Intelligence and Beauty itself, why art thou a slave of lust and impurity ?

सर्वभूतेषु चात्मानं सर्वभूतानि चात्मनि ॥
मुनेर्जानत आश्चर्यं ममत्वमनुवर्त्तते ॥ ५ ॥

5. Wonderful it is, that even in the sage who sees the Self in all beings and all beings in the Self, there should be left any sense of "mine."

आस्थितः परमाद्वैतं मोक्षार्थेऽपि व्यवस्थितः ॥
आश्चर्यं कामवशगो विकलः केलिशिक्षया ॥ ६ ॥

6. Wonderful it is, that even one abiding in supreme unity and intent upon the object of release, should be subject to desire and agitated by sensual delights.

उद्भूतं ज्ञानदुर्मित्रमवधार्यातिदुर्बलः ॥
आश्चर्यं काममाकांक्षेत्कालमंतमनुश्रितः ॥ ७ ॥

7. Knowing the nature of wisdom's great enemy, wonderful it is to see the sage who sees his end approaching, cherishing love for sensual objects.

इहामुत्र विरक्तस्य नित्यानित्यविवेकिनः ॥
आश्चर्यं मोक्षकामस्य मोक्षादेव विभीषिका ॥८॥

8. Wonderful it is, that even to one who is un-attached to objects both of this world and of the next, who discriminates the eternal from the non-eternal, and who is bent upon emancipation, there should be fear from that very emancipation ![1]

धीरस्तु भोज्यमानोऽपि पीड्यमानोऽपि सर्वदा ॥
आत्मानं केवलं पश्यन्न तुष्यति न कुप्यति ॥ ९ ॥

9. Feasted or spurned, the sage of controlled mind who sees only his own Self, is neither pleased nor angry.

चेष्टमानं शरीरं स्वं पश्यत्यन्यशरीरवत् ॥
संस्तवे चापि निन्दायां कथं क्षुभ्येन्महाशयः ॥१०॥

10. Seeing his own body acting as if it were another's, how should one of great soul be disturbed by praise or censure !

मायामात्रमिदं विश्वं पश्यन्विगतकौतुकः ॥
अपि सन्निहिते मृत्यौ कथं त्रस्यति धीरधीः ॥११॥

11. Seeing the world as an illusion, with all curiosity gone, how can the man of controlled mind fear even the approach of death !

निःस्पृहं मानसं यस्य नैराश्येऽपि महात्मनः ॥
तस्यात्मज्ञानतृप्तस्य तुलना केन जायते ॥ १२ ॥

12. The great soul whose mind is without desire for even that which is beyond desire, who finds peace in Self-realization, what is there with which he can be compared ?

---

(1) Emancipation here means release from objects of the world. Like the silkworm which shuts itself in a cocoon of its own making, man shuts himself in this cocoon of belief in the reality of the world and even though the Sastra tells him that happiness lies in breaking through it, he dreads it.

स्वभावादेव जानानो इदयमेतन्न किंचन ॥
इदं ग्राह्यमिदं त्याज्यं स किं पश्यति धीरधीः ॥१३॥

13.   The man of controlled mind who knows the visible to be in its nature a mere nothing, sees not this to be attained nor that to be avoided.

अंतस्त्यक्तकषायस्य निर्द्वंदस्य निराशिषः ॥
यदृच्छयागतो भोगो न दुःखाय न तुष्टये ॥ १४ ॥

14   To one who has washed off all internal impurity who is free from all notion of diversity, and who has arisen above hope, enjoyment of objects coming in their natural course is neither pleasurable nor painful. [1]

CHAPTER 4.

The Disciple's experience described.

हंतात्मज्ञस्य धीरस्य खेलतो भोगलीलया ॥ .
न हि संसारवाहीकैर्मूढैः सह समानता ॥ १ ॥

1.   Says the Disciple :—O joy ! there is no comparison between the sage who knows his Self, and sports in the world of sense, and those beasts of burden who are attached to the yoke of the world.

यत्पदं प्रेप्सवो दीनाः शक्राद्याः सर्वदेवताः ॥
अहो तत्रस्थितो योगी न हर्षमुपगच्छति ॥ २ ॥

---

(1) Says Prahlada to Indra—" Without attachment, without pride, without desire and hope, free from all bonds and dissociated from every thing, I am passing my time in great happiness, seeing the appearance and disappearance of all created objects. For one that is possessed of wisdom, who is self-restrained who is contented, who is without hope or desire, and who beholds all things with the light of Self knowledge, there is no trouble, no anxiety, O Indra." (Mahabharata, Moksha Dharma, Chap. 222. Verses, 30-31.

2. Oh ! The Yogi though abiding in that which Indra and other gods long for in vain, is not elated.

तज्ज्ञस्य पुण्यपापाभ्यां स्पर्शो ह्यंतनं जायते ॥

न ह्याकाशस्य धूमेन दृश्यमानापि संगतिः ॥ ३ ॥

3. Good and evil touch not the inner Self of him who knows That. The ether (Akasa) though appearing to be covered with smoke, is in truth untouched by it.

आत्मैवेदं जगत्सर्वं ज्ञातं येन महात्मना ॥

यदृच्छया वर्त्तमानं तं निषेद्धुं क्षमेत कः ॥ ४ ॥

4. Who is there to prohibit from moving as he choses, the man of great soul who has known that all this is the Self alone ?

आब्रह्मस्तंबपर्यंते भूतग्रामे चतुर्विधे ॥

विज्ञस्यैव हि सामर्थ्यमिच्छानिच्छाविवर्जने ॥ ५ ॥

5. In the world composed of the four kinds of creatures from Brahmá to a blade of grass, it is the knower of the Self alone who has the strength to renounce the pleasurable and the painful.

आत्मानमद्वयं कश्चिज्जानाति जगदीश्वरम् ॥

यद्वेत्ति तत्स कुरुते न भयं तस्य कुत्रचित् ॥ ६ ॥

6. One amongst thousands only[1], knows his own Self, free from duality, as the One Lord of the world. Having known this, he acts in the world under the impulse of Karma which is already commenced to bear fruit (like a potter's wheel revolving even after the hand which set it in motion is withdrawn). For such a one there is no fear on any side.

---

(1) i. e., the Jiwanmukta.

CHAPTER 5.

The four kinds of absorption into the Atma.

न ते संगोऽस्ति केनापि किं शुद्धस्त्यक्तुमिच्छसि ॥
संघातविलयं कुर्वन्नेवमेव लयं व्रज ॥ १ ॥

1. Says the master.—No attachment to anything whatsoever is thine ; pure art thou, what dost thou wish to renounce ?   Merging this aggregate [1] into the Atma, do thou thus find absorption in thy own Self.

उदेति भवतो विश्वं वारिधेरिव बुद्बुदः ॥
इति ज्ञात्वैकमात्मानमेवमेव लयं व्रज ॥ २ ॥

2. The world appears in thee like bubbles in the ocean.   Thus knowing the Self to be One, do thou thus find absorption in thy own self.

प्रत्यक्षमप्यवस्तुत्वाद्विश्वं नास्त्यमले त्वयि ॥
रज्जुसर्प इव व्यक्तमेवमेव लयं व्रज ॥ ॥ ३

3. The world though present to the senses is in reality not in thee, the Pure.   It appears like the snake in the rope.   Do thou thus find absorption in thy own Self.

समदुःखसुखः पूर्ण आशानैराश्ययोः समः ॥
समजीवितमृत्युः सन्नेवमेव लयं व्रज ॥ ४ ॥

4. The same in pleasure and pain, full, equal in hope and disappointment, equal in life and death, do thou thus find absorption in thy own Self.

---

(1) Of the body, the senses, the mind, the intellect and the vital airs.

CHAPTER. 6.

In Truth there is no emanation nor absorption in the Atma.

आकाशवदनंतोऽहं घटवत्प्राकृतं जगत् ॥
इति ज्ञानं तथैतस्य न त्यागो न ग्रहो लयः ॥१॥

1. Says the Disciple :—As space unbounded am I, like unto a jar is this world, matter-wrought. This is knowledge certain (taught by the Vedanta and realized under the direction of the teacher). There is here no attainment, no relinquishment, no absorption.

महोदधिरिवाहं स प्रपंचो वीचिसन्निभः ॥
इति ज्ञानं तथैतस्य न त्यागो न ग्रहो लयः ॥२॥

2. I am the great Ocean in which the world is a wave. This is knowledge, certain and realized. There is here no attainment, no realinquishment, no absorption.

अहं स शुक्तिसंकाशो रूपवद्दिश्वकल्पना ॥
इति ज्ञानं तथैतस्य न त्यागो न ग्रहो लयः ॥३॥

3. I am that mother of pearl on which this world is superimposed like silver. This is knowledge certain and realized. There is here no attainment, no relinquishment, no absorption.

अहं वा सर्वभूतेषु सर्वभूताऽन्यथो मयि ॥
इति ज्ञानं तथैतस्य न त्यागो न ग्रहो लयः ॥४॥

4. I am either in all beings or all beings are in me. This is knowledge, certain and realized. There is here no attainment, no relinquishment, no absorption.

CHAPTER 7.

Realization of Atma in worldly life.

मय्यनंतमहांभोधौ विश्वपोत इतस्ततः ॥
भ्रमाति स्वांतवातेन न ममास्त्यसहिष्णुता ॥ १ ॥

1. Says the Disciple :—In Me, the limitless Ocean, the bark of the world tosses about, impelled by the wind of mind, but it affects Me not.

मय्यनंतमहांभोधौ जगद्वीचिः स्वभावतः ॥
उदेतु वास्तमायातु न मे वृद्धिर्नं च क्षतिः ॥ २ ॥

2. In Me, the limitless Ocean, let the wave of the world rise or vanish of itself ; I suffer no increase, no decrease thereby.

मय्यनंतमहांभोधौ विश्वं नाम विकल्पना ॥
अतिशांतो निराकार एतदेवाहमास्थितः ॥ ३ ॥

3. On Me, the limitless Ocean, the world is merely superimposed. Highly tranquil, formless am I ; thus indeed do I remain.

नात्मा भावेषु नो भावस्त्रानंते निरंजने ॥
इत्यसक्तोऽस्पृहः शांत एतदेवाहमास्थितः ॥ ४ ॥

4. The Atmá is not in the visible, nor is the visible in That which is unlimited and unblemished. Thus free from attachment, free for desire and tranquil, do I abide in my own Self.

अहो चिन्मात्रमेवाहमिंद्रजालोपमं जगत् ॥
अतो मम कथं कुत्र हेयोपादेयकल्पना ॥ ५ ॥

5. Oh ! I am Intelligence itself. The world is a juggler's show. How can then there be any notion of adoption or relinquishment here.

CHAPTER 8.

The Nature of Release and Bondage.

तदा बंधो यदा चित्तं किंचिद्वांछति शोचति ॥
किंचिन्मुंचति गृह्णाति किंचिद्दृष्यति कुप्यति ॥१॥

1. Says the Teacher :—Then is bondage, when the mind wishes for anything, grieves at anything, renounces anything, takes anything, feels unhappy in anything, or is angry at anything.

तदा मुक्तिर्यदा चित्तं न वांछति न शोचति ॥
न मुंचति न गृह्णाति न हृष्यति न कुप्यति ॥२॥

2. Then is release, when the mind wishes not, grieves not, abandons not, grasps not, feels not happy or unhappy at anything.

तदा बंधो यदा चित्तं सक्तं कास्वपि दृष्टिषु ॥
तदा मोक्षो यदा चित्तमसक्तं सर्वदृष्टिषु ॥ ३ ॥

3. Then is bondage, when the mind is attached to any condition whatever. Then is release, when the mind is unattached to all conditions whatsoever.

यदा नाहं तदा मोक्षो यदाहं बंधनं तदा ॥
मत्वेति हेलया किंचिन्मा गृहाण विमुंच मा ॥४॥

4. When there is no "I" there is release, where

there is " I " there is bondage. Knowing this, do not take or avoid anything in life.[1]

CHAPTER 9.
Eight verses on Concernedness[2].

कृताकृते च द्वंद्वानि कदा शांतानि कस्य वा ॥
एवं ज्ञात्वेह निर्वेदाद्भव त्यागपरोऽव्रती ॥ १ ॥

1. Says the Teacher :—Things done and not done, and pairs of opposites[3] when are they set at rest, and for whom ? Having known this, even here be thou, through unconcernedness intent on renunciation and free from all attachment whatsoever.

कस्यापि तात धन्यस्य लोकचेष्टावलोकनात् ॥
जीवितेच्छा बुभुक्षा च बुभुत्सोपशमं गताः ॥२॥

2. Who, my child, is the fortunate man, in whom, by dint of gazing at the world-show, lust of life, love of enjoyment and thirst for knowledge are set at rest?

अनित्यं सर्वमेवेदं तापत्रितयदूषितम् ॥
असारं निंदितं हेयमिति निश्चित्य शाम्यति ॥३॥

---

(1) Speaking of the indications of the knowers of Brahma—says Rishi Jaigishavya. "Having cut asunder all knots of the heart, they roam about at pleasure. None is related to them nor are they related to any one. None is their enemy nor are they enemies of any one. Above praise and blame they are always at peace, ever bent upon the good of others." Mahabharata—Speaking of Rishi Narada Krishna said. The practice of virtue does not beget in him that egotism which burns one's self. His actions correspond with his thoughts, therefore he is universally worshipped. Ever unattached to anything he looks like one attached. He never passes his time fruitlessly. His senses are under complete control. He never prays into the defects of others but is always mindful of his own. Acquisition of objects of the world does not elate him, nor does their loss depress him. Of firm intellect, of an unconcerned disposition, he is worshipped everywhere."

(2) Nirveda.
(3) Pleasure and pain, gain and loss, good and evil, heaven and hell, etc.

3. Impermanent is all this, undermined by the threefold misery [1], void of essence, full of blemish, fit to be cast away. Having realized this, one goes to peace.

कोऽसौ कालो वयः किं वा यत्र द्वंद्वानि नो नृणाम् ॥
तान्युपेक्ष्य यथाप्राप्तवर्ती सिद्धिमवाप्नुयात् ॥ ४ ॥

4. What is the time, what the age when pairs of opposites [2] do not exist for man ? Taking no heed of these, doing whatever offers, one attains to perfection.

नाना मतं महर्षीणां साधूनां योगिनां तथा ॥
दृष्ट्वा निर्वेदमापन्नः को न शाम्यति मानवः ॥५॥

5. Manifold are the doctrines of the great Sages, of Saints and Yogis as well. Having seen this and gained unconcernedness, what man may not come to peace ?

कृत्वा मूर्तिपरिज्ञानं चैतन्यस्य नर्किंगुरुः ॥
निर्वेदसमतायुक्त्या यस्तारयति संसृतेः ॥ ६ ॥

6. Having gained full realization of the Conscious Essence by the practice of unconcernedness and equanimity, he who is an excellent teacher becomes a saviour of the world.

पश्य भूतविकारांस्त्वं भूतमात्रान् यथार्थतः ॥
तत्क्षणाद्वंधनिर्मुक्तः स्वरूपस्थो भविष्यसि ॥७॥

7. As soon as thou seest that the modifications of the elements [3] are nothing in truth but the basic ele-

---

(1) *Adhyatmika, adhidaivika adhibhautika i. e.,* from one's own self, from the gods (*i. e., karma*) and from physical nature.

(2) Pleasure and pain, heat and cold, &c.

(3) The world as composed of the five elements.

ments themselves, that very instant, freed from bondage, thou shalt abide in thy own nature.

वासना एव संसार इति सर्वा विमुंच ताः ॥
तत्त्यागो वासनात्यागात्स्थितिरद्य यथा तथा ॥८॥

8. The world is nothing but *vasana*,[1] do thou
disperse all these. The renunciation of the former[2]
follows on the renuciation of the latter[3] As his condition is now, thus he remains[4].

CHAPTER 10.

Eight verses on Quietude.

विहाय वैरिणं काममर्थं चानर्थं संकुलम् ॥
धर्ममप्येतयोर्हेतुं सर्वत्रानादरं कुरु ॥ १ ॥

1. Says the Teacher:—Having forsaken Desire, the
enemy, and woeful lust of wealth, as well as dharma (re-
ligous merit)[5] which gives rise to both, do thou cast off
attachment and be indifferent to everything.

---

(1) The aggregate of accumulated mental (and emotional) impressions.
(2) *i. e*, of the world.
(3) *i. e.*, of the *vasanas.*
(4) *i. e.*, he lives in the world for working out the remainder of his
Karma.

(5) The Vedanta holds that dharma (virtue) is as much a mental state as
any other emotion concerning life in the world or hereafter and that for
one who seeks emancipation, complete suppression of all emotion is the
only course possible. The parting words of Narada to Suka therefore
were—"Do thou relinquish dharma—virtue and adharma—vice, as well as
truth and untruth. Having renounced both truth and untruth, do thou
renounce that by which thou hast renounced these. Renounce dharma by
suppression of the action of the mind, adharma by having no vicious
thoughts, truth and untruth by knowledge and knowledge by ascertainment
of the supreme." In the Absolute, virtue, vice, duty or the absence
thereof finds no place. In the ordinary condition of life there are however
two kinds of dharma-*sakama* and *niskama* (*i. e.*, done with or without motive of reward). The former leads to the sansara, the latter prepares the
way for moksha. Desire and lust of wealth arise from the former. In the
final stage of *gyana* the latter has also to be renounced.

स्वप्नेंद्रजालवत्पश्य दिनानि त्रीणि पंच वा ॥

मित्रक्षेत्रधनागारदारादायादिसंपदः ॥ २ ॥

2. Know friends, lands, wealth, houses, wives, and affluence to be like things in a dream or a juggler's show, lasting but three or five days.

यत्र यत्र भवेत्तृष्णा संसारं विद्धि तत्र वै ॥

प्रौढवैराग्यमाश्रित्य वीततृष्णः सुखी भव ॥ ३ ॥

3. Know the world to be there where is desire. Do thou betake thyself to firm non-attachment, be free from desire and happy. [1]

तृष्णामात्रात्मको बंधस्तन्नाशो मोक्ष उच्यते ॥

भवासंसक्तिमात्रेण प्राप्तितुष्टिर्मुहुर्मुहुः ॥ ४ ॥

4. Bondage consists only in desire, its destruction is release. Non-attachment to the visible, gradually leads to the happiness following realization of Self.

त्वमेकश्चेतनः शुद्धो जडं विश्वमसत्तथा ॥

अविद्यापि न किंचित्सा का बुभुत्सा तथापि ते ॥५॥

5. Thou art One, Intelligent, and Pure, the world is devoid of Intelligence and false. *Avidyá* [1] itself is nothing, what thirst of knowledge can there be for thee ?

राज्यं सुताः कलत्राणि शरीराणि सुखानि च ॥

संसक्तस्यापि नष्टानि तव जन्मनि जन्मनि ॥ ६ ॥

---

(1) Says Vyása :—"Running after sensual delights why dost thou not betake thyself to renunciation. Fool thou art that seest only the honey (at the top of the hill), not the abyss below. Fickle minded as thou art, be thou firm, fool as thou art, do thou betake thyself to wisdom. Agitated as thou art, be thou now at peace—devoid of knowledge of self as thou art, do thou be possessed of self-knowledge. Arise awake, ever on the alert are thy enemies within thee watching for opportunity to destroy thee: Why dost thou not hasten to destroy them"—(Mahabharata Moksha Dharma, Chap. 310).

6. Kingdoms, sons, wives, bodies and pleasures, have all been lost to thee, birth after birth, even though thou wast attached to them.

अलमर्थेन कामेन सुकृतेनापि कर्मणा ॥

एभ्यः संसारकान्तारे न विश्रान्तमभून्मनः ॥ ७ ॥

7. Enough then, of love of wealth, desire and even good deeds. In none of these did the mind find rest in this forest of the world.

कृतं न कति जन्मानि कायेन मनसा गिरा ॥

दुःखमायासदं कर्म तदद्याप्युपरम्यताम् ॥ ८ ॥

8. For how many incarnations did'st thou not engage in action with body, mind and speech, all resulting in nothing but trouble ? Do thou now cease from action.

CHAPTER II.

Eight verses on Wisdom.

भावाभावविकारश्च स्वभावादिति निश्चयी ॥

निर्विकारो गतक्लेशः सुखेनैवोपशाम्यति ॥ १ ॥

1. Says the teacher : —Existence and non-existence with their modifications are all due to the nature of things. Knowing this for certain, undisturbed, and free from pain, one finds peace easily.

ईश्वरः सर्वनिर्माता नेहान्य इति निश्चयी ॥

अन्तर्गलितसर्वाशः शान्तः क्वापि न सज्जते ॥ २ ॥

2. It is God who is the Creator of all. There is none other here. Knowing this for certain, with desire set at rest within, one finds peace and is attached to nothing whatever.

आपदः संपदः काले दैवादेवेति निश्चयी ॥
तृप्तः स्वस्थेंद्रियो नित्यं न वांछति न शोचति ॥३॥

3. Past action alone brings affluence and misery, each in its own turn. Knowing this, contented and with all organs of sense controlled, one desires nothing, nor feels grieved at anything.

सुखदुःखे जन्ममृत्यू दैवादेवेति निश्चयी ॥
साध्यादर्शी निरायासः कुर्वन्नपि न लिप्यते ॥४॥

4. Pleasure and pain, birth and death are due to past Karma. Knowing this for certain, as well as his inability to alter it, freed from anxiety, one is not stained even though engaged in action.

चिंतया जायते दुःखं नान्यथेहेति निश्चयी ॥
तया हीनः सुखी शांतः सर्वत्र गलितस्पृहः ॥५॥

5. Care alone breeds sorrow, nothing else does. Knowing this, above care, and happy, one finds peace and is free from all attachment whatever.

नाहं देहो न मे देहो बोधोऽहमिति निश्चयी ॥
कैवल्यमिव संप्राप्तो न स्मरत्यकृतं कृतम् ॥ ६ ॥

6. "I am not this body, nor is this body mine. I am intelligence itself. " One who knows this for certain,

attains to union [1] and does not remember what he has done or not done.

आब्रह्मस्तंबपर्यंतमहमेवेति निश्चयी ॥
निर्विकल्पः शुचिः शांतः प्राप्ताप्राप्तविनिर्वृतः ॥७॥

7. " From Brahmá down to a blade of grass, I am verily all this, " one who knows this for certain, is free from all conflicting thoughts, pure, at peace and indifferent to what is attained and what is not attained.

नानाश्चर्यमिदं विश्वं न किंचिदिति निश्चयी ॥
निर्वासनः स्फूर्तिमात्रो न किंचिदिव शाम्यति ॥८॥

8. " This diversified and wonderful world is verily nothing." Knowing this, free from desire and specific cognition, one finds his rest.

CHAPTER 12.

Eight verses on realization of the same by the disciple.

कायकृत्यासहः पूर्वे ततो वाग्विस्तरासहः ॥
अथ चिंतासहस्तस्मादेवमेवाह मास्थितः ॥ १ ॥

1. Says the Disciple :—First I felt disinclined to bodily exertion, then to length of speech and finally to mental exertion. Even thus do I stand.

प्रीत्याभावेन शब्दादेरह्रद्यत्वेन चात्मनः ॥
विक्षेपैकाग्रहृदय एवमेवाहमास्थितः ॥ २ ॥

2. Because of sound [2] &c., being no object of affection to me ; and because of the Átma being no object of

---

[1] With the átma.
[2] Objects of sense.

cognition by the senses, my mind is free from distraction and is one-pointed. Even thus do I stand.[1]

समाध्यासादिविक्षिप्तौ व्यवहारः समाधये ॥
एवं विलोक्य नियममेवमेवाहमास्थितः ॥ ३ ॥

3. The practice conducive to Samadhi is the equableness in the distraction caused by superimposition and the rest. Knowing this to be the rule, thus do I stand.[2]

हेयोपादेयविरहादेवं हर्षविषादयोः ॥
अभावाद्य हे ब्रह्मन्नेवमेवाहमास्थितः ॥ ४ ॥

4. Having nothing to gain or lose, having no joy or sorrow, thus, O Knower of Brahman, do I stand.

आश्रमानाश्रमं ध्यानं चित्तस्वीकृतवर्जनम् ॥
विकल्पं मम वीक्ष्यैतैरेवमेवाहमास्थितः ॥ ५ ॥

5. The rules of the order, the condition of those who have left their order, meditation and the relinquishment of what has been acquired, knowing all these to be so many distractions to me, thus do I abide in my own Self.

कर्मानुष्ठानमज्ञानाद्यथैवोपरमस्तथा ॥
बुध्वा सम्यगिदं तत्त्वमेवमेवाहमास्थितः ॥ ६ ॥

---

(1) The sense is that the átma being beyond mind, is not an object of meditation and there is thus for me no distraction due to such mental contemplation. On the contrary I abide in my own self, free from all thoughts, all distraction.

(2) Samadhi is resorted to for removal of the wrong notion of 'I am the body' or 'I am the doer' and the distraction caused thereby. But when the sage has realized that he is not the body nor the doer or enjoyer of action, what need is there for him to engage in Samadhi?

6. The performance of action is as much due to ignorance (avidyá) as the cessation thereof. Knowing this well, thus do I stand.

अचिंत्यं चिंत्यमानोऽपि चिंतारूपं भजत्यसौ ॥
त्यक्त्वा तद्भावनं तस्मादेवमेवाहमास्थितः ॥ ७ ॥

7. Meditating upon that which is not an object of meditation, one only betakes himself to an action of the mind. Having relinquished this notion, I now stand where I am [1].

एवमेव कृतं येन स कृतार्थो भवेदसौ ॥
एवमेव स्वभावो यः स कृतार्थो भवेदसौ ॥ ८ ॥

8. He who has accomplished this has achieved all that had to be achieved, what need be said of one who by nature is such ? [2]

CHAPTER 13.

Seven verses on Happiness.

अकिंचनभवं स्वास्थ्यं कौपीनत्वेऽपि दुर्लभम् ॥
त्यागादाने विहायास्मादहमासे यथा सुखम् ॥ १ ॥

---

(1) 'I am Brahman' is as much an action of the mind as 'I am the body' and must be suppressed like any other thought.

(2) This chapter inculcates once more that most difficult, but none the less, the most important lesson of Vedanta, viz., that for the knower of Self, there is nothing to be done. All action, study and meditation cease when that which was to be attained has been realized. The man of wisdom having therefore studied books treating of knowledge of self and meditated upon them, throws them aside like the seeker of grain does the chaff. For such a person there is no necessity of doing any thing. Like the ocean with all billows set at rest, he has found his rest in his own self. There are two kinds of renunciation one of the object of cognition and the other of the sense of I am the cognizer. The sage who has known his atmá is above both.

1. Says the Disciple :—That tranquillity of mind which results from the absence of all attachment whatever, is difficult to attain even when there is the slightest attachment to the smallest object, such as a piece of cloth used for tying round the waist. Having therefore given up both search and relinquishment, I live happy.

कुत्रापि खेदः कायस्य जिह्वा कुत्र पि विद्यते ॥
मनः कुत्रापि तत्त्यक्त्वा पुरुषार्थे स्थितः सुखम् ॥२॥

2. There is trouble of the body somewhere,[1] trouble of the mind somewhere,[2] and trouble of speech somewhere ;[3] having relinquished all these, do I live happy in my own Self.

कृतं किमपि नैव स्यादिति संचिंत्य तत्त्वतः ॥
यदा यत्कर्तुमायाति तत्कृत्वासे यथा सुखम् ॥३॥

3. Nothing done by the body and the organs of sense is done by the Atma. Having known this truth, I do what comes before me and am happy.

कर्मनैष्कर्म्यनिर्बंधभावा देहस्थयोगिनः ॥
संयोगायोगविरहादहमासे यथा सुखम् ॥ ४ ॥

4. Inclination to action or cessation of action is for the yogi who ~~has~~ attached to the body. Having relinquished both attachment and non-attachment, I am happy.

---

(1) In fasts and penance.
(2) In study.
(3) In repetition of sacred Mantras.

अर्थानर्थौ न मे स्थिरया गतया न शयनेन वा ॥

तिष्ठन् गच्छन् स्वपन् तस्मादहमासे यथा सुखम् ॥५॥

5. Sitting, going or sleeping I gain and lose nothing. Therefore standing, moving or sleeping, I live
happy.

स्वपतो नास्ति मे हानिः सिद्धिर्यत्नवतो न वा ॥

नाशोल्लासौ विहायास्मदहमासे यथा सुखम् ॥६॥

6. Sleeping I lose nothing, striving I gain nothing.
Having therefore relinquished gain and loss, I am happy.

सुखादिरूपानियमं भावेवालोक्य भूरिशः ॥

शुभाशुभे विहायास्मादहमासे यथा सुखम् ॥ ७ ॥

7. Having repeatedly felt the instability of both
pleasure and pain in each successive birth, I have
renounced both good and evil and am happy[1].

CHAPTER 14.

Four verses on the disciple's condition of bliss.

प्रकृत्या शून्यचित्तो यः प्रमादाद्भावभावनः ॥

निद्रितो बोधित इव क्षीणसंसरणो हि सः ॥१॥

1. Says the Disciple :—He becomes verily world-
exhausted whose mind has naturally become vacant of
all thought, who becomes conscious of external existence only through heedlessness, and who though asleep
is in reality awake [1].

---

(1) Says Vashiṣṭha to Rama. "Do thou make thy mind vacant of all
thought and function in the outside world to a limited extent only and be

क धनानि क मित्राणि क मे विषयदस्यवः ॥
क शास्त्रं क च विज्ञानं यदा मे गलिता स्पृहा ॥२॥

2. For me where are riches, friends and those thieves known as object of sense, where is *shastra* or its knowledge, when all desire has ceased to exist in me ?

विज्ञाते साक्षिपुरुषे परमात्मनि चेश्वरे ॥
नैराश्ये बंधमोक्षेच न चिंता मुक्तये मम ॥ ३ ॥

3. When I have realized the Witness, the Supreme Self, the Lord, and when all longing for release and bondage has gone, there is no anxiety for emancipation.

अंतर्विकल्पशून्यस्य बहिः स्वच्छंदचारिणः ॥
भ्रांतस्येव दशास्तास्तास्तादृशा एव जानते ॥४॥

4. The condition of one whose mind has ceased to act, but who roams about in the world like one under an illusion, can only be known by one like himself. [2]

---

inside as if in deep sleep. Thus will thou be free from all sorrow. Make thy deep slumber thy waking condition and thy waking condition thy deep slumber—That which remains in the union of the two, is thy own Pure Self." Or as said by Sri Krishna in the Gita " That which is night to all other creatures, is day to the sage whose mind has been brought under complete control, that in which other creatures are awake, is night to one who sees his own self."

(2) One of the questions which doubles most readers of Vedanta is :— " How shall I live, if I give up all sense of egoism." The answer is that complete cessation of all sense of the I in the body &c. is possible only in the final stage of Gyana which is seedless meditation.—Nirvikalpa Samadhi. In the previous stages such sense of I becomes attenuated, but every step towards such attenuation is a step forward. This is the experience of all Vedantins past and present.

CHAPTER 15.

Twenty verses on knowledge of the Self.

यथा तथोपदेशेन कृतार्थः सत्त्वबुद्धिमान् ॥
आजीवमपि जिज्ञासुः परस्तत्र विमुह्यति ॥ १ ॥

1. Says the Teacher :—The man of pure intellect achieves his object by even instruction imparted in an accidental manner, but to one of impure intellect, even repeated instruction does not prevent from going astray.

मोक्षो विषयवैरस्यं बंधो वैषयिको रसः ॥
एतावदेव विज्ञानं यथेच्छसि तथा कुरु ॥ २ ॥

2. Distaste for objects of sense is release, love of objects of sense is bondage. This is knowledge, do thou act as thou chosest.

वाग्मिप्राज्ञमहोद्योगं जनं मूकजडाल्सम् ॥
करोति तत्त्वबोधोऽयमतस्त्यक्तो बुभुक्षुभिः ॥ ३ ॥

3. This knowledge makes the eloquent mute, the wise unwise, the active inactive. Therefore lovers of objects of sense shun it.[1]

_____

(1) It is not that the eloquent are deprived of their power of speech, or the wise become fools, or the busy inactive by acquiring Brahma Vidyá, but that their activity which was formerly directed towards the world of sense, is now directed towards self-realization. Had the object of the Vedanta been to make men idiotic idlers, it would not have given us teachers like Krishna, Bishma, Vyasa and Sankara. On the contrary the knower of Brahman, though himself released, yet comes into the world as often as is required, to fulfil the moral law. The Vedanta does not tell the sage to go about in the world behaving like a child or an idiot or like one in a dream. But it requires that like a child he should be simple and guileless in his ways, and should have no thought of the past or the future and should value things of the world like those of a dream. All that it does is to strike at the root of all sense of egotism, all pride of learning, possession and race, in the earlier stages, and of all sense of " I " and " mine " in the body and its surroundings, later on. The Bhagwadgitá and the Yogaváshishtha, two of the most authoritative books of Vedanta, are the works of men who

5

न त्वं देहो न ते देहो भोक्ता कर्त्ता न वा भवान् ॥
चिद्रूपोऽसि सदा साक्षी निरपेक्षः सुखं चर ॥४॥

4. Thou art not the body, nor is the body thine, nor art thou an actor or enjoyer. Thou art Intelligence itself, the Ever Witness, the Ever Free. Do thou roam happy.

रागद्वेषौ मनोधर्मौ न मनस्ते कदाचन ॥
निर्विकल्पोऽसिबोधात्मा निर्विकारः सुखं चर ॥५॥

5. Attachment and aversion are conditions of the mind, the mind is never thine. Free from all distraction, thou art Intelligence itself, without change, do thou be happy.

सर्वभूतेषु चात्मानं सर्वभूतानि चात्मनि ॥
विज्ञाय निरहंकारो निर्ममस्त्वं सुखी भव ॥ ६ ॥

6. Knowing thy own self to be in all beings, and all beings in thy own self, free from all sense of "I" or "mine," do thou be happy.

विश्वं स्फुरति यत्रेदं तरंगा इव सागरे ॥
तत्त्वमेव न संदेहश्चिन्मूर्ते विज्वरो भव ॥ ७ ॥

7. That in which the world rises like waves in the ocean, that verily art thou, O thou Supreme Intelligence, be thou free from all fever.

---

were as active for the good of society as in realization of the Self within them as the Self of all. In the final stages of gyána, action of either the mind or the body becomes well nigh impossible. As said by Krishna in the Gitá, "for the aspirant after yoga action is necessary. For one who has reached it cessation of action is necessary." But that is not the stage of work, but of absorption in the Self, after which the body does not last but for a few days. A misapprehension of this truth has led many into pitfalls and produced results never contemplated by the Shastras.

श्रद्धस्व तात श्रद्धस्व नात्र मोहं कुरुष्व भोः ॥
ज्ञानस्वरूपो भगवानात्मा त्वं प्रकृतेः परः ॥ ८ ॥

8. Have faith, my son, have faith, do not delude thyself here. Thou art Intelligence, thou art the Lord, thou the Self, beyond Prakriti.

गुणैः संवेष्टितो देहस्तिष्ठत्यायाति याति च ॥
आत्मा न गंता नागंता किमेनमनु शोचसि ॥ ९ ॥

9. The body covered with the organs of sense &c., comes and goes. The Átmá (Self) neither comes nor goes, why dost thou grieve for it (the Átmá).

देहस्तिष्ठतु कल्पांतं गच्छत्वद्यैव वा पुनः ॥
क्व वृद्धिः क च वा हानिस्तव चिन्मात्ररूपिणः ॥ १० ॥

10. Let the body last till the end of a Kalpa (cycle) or go this very day, what increase or decrease is there in thee, the very Self of intelligence ?

त्वय्यनंतमहांभोधौ विश्ववीचिः स्वभावतः ॥
उदेतु वास्तमायातु न ते वृद्धिर्न वा क्षतिः ॥ ११ ॥

11. Let the waves of the world rise or fall in Thee, the limitless ocean, there is neither increase nor decrease in Thee.

तात चिन्मात्ररूपोऽसि न ते भिन्नमिदं जगत् ॥
अतः कस्य कथं कुत्र हेयोपादेय कल्पना ॥ १२ ॥

12. Thou art, my son, Intelligence itself. The world is no other than thee. Therefore whose and whence is here desire or aversion ?

एकस्मिन्नव्यये शांते चिदाकाशेऽमले त्वयि ॥

कुतो जन्म कुतो कर्म कुतोऽहंकार एव च ॥१३॥

13. In Thee, the One, free from decay, Bliss itself, the Absolute Intelligence, the Ever Pure, where is birth or action or the sense of the " I" ?

यत्त्वं पश्यसि तत्रैकस्त्वमेव प्रतिभाससे ॥

किं पृथक् भासते स्वर्णात्कटकांगदनूपुरम् ॥१४॥

14. What thou seest, there thou alone art seen. Are bangles, armlets or trinkets other than gold ?

अयं सोऽहमयं नाहं विभागमिति संत्यज ॥

सर्वमात्मेति निश्चित्य निःसंकल्प सुखी भव ॥१५॥

15. "I am this," "I am not this", do thou leave off this sense of separateness. Realizing that all this is Átmá, be thou free of all mental conditions and be happy.

तवैवाज्ञानतो विश्वं त्वमेकः परमार्थतः ॥

त्वत्तोऽन्यो नास्ति संसारी नासंसारी च कश्चन ॥१६॥

16. This world springs verily from thy own illusion. In truth thou alone art one. There is no other embodied Self (Jiva) than thee, nor one who is beyond the Sansara.

भ्रांतिमात्रमिदं विश्वं न किंचिदिति निश्चयी ॥

निर्वासनः स्फूर्तिमात्रो न किंचिदिव शाम्यति ॥१७॥

17. This world is but a delusion. One who knows this, finds peace ; all longing gone, he abides in supreme consciousness and finds rest as if in nothing.* [1]

---

* *i.e.*, Freed of all specific cognition whatever.

एक एव भवांभोधावासीदास्ति भविष्यति ॥
न ते बंधोऽस्ति मोक्षो वा कृतकृत्यः सुखं चर ॥१८॥

18. In the great ocean of the visible, One alone is, was and shall be. For thee there is no release, no bondage, with all desires fulfilled, be thou happy.

मा संकल्पविकल्पाभ्यां चित्तं क्षोभय चिन्मय ॥
उपशाम्य सुखं तिष्ठ स्वात्मन्यानंदविग्रहे ॥१९॥

19. O thou Supreme Intelligence ! Do not trouble thy mind with conflicting thoughts. Do thou find rest and be happy in thy own self, the embodiment of bliss.

त्यजैव ध्यानं सर्वत्र मा किंचिद्धृदि धारय ॥
आत्मा त्वं मुक्त एवासि किं विमृश्य करिष्यसि ॥२०॥

20. Give up all meditation, carry nothing in thy heart. Thou art verily the Self, free from bondage, what shall meditation do for thee ?

CHAPTER 16.

Eleven verses on special instruction.

आचक्ष्व शृणु वा तात नानाशास्त्राण्यनेकशः ॥
तथापि न तव स्वास्थ्यं सर्वविस्मरणादृते ॥ १ ॥

1. Says the Teacher :—Thou may'st, my son, discourse upon repeatedly, or hear diverse Sastras, but there is no peace for thee but through universal forgetfulness [1].

---

(1) The last word of the Brahma Vidyá is *Silence.* " This Atma is silence" (Santoyam Atmá). It is in silence that you realize that before which even the sovereignty of the three worlds appears like a blade of grass. All instruction, all knowledge, whether of this or the world to come,

भोगं कर्म समाधिं वा कुरु विज्ञ तथापि ते ॥
चित्तं निरस्तसर्वाशमत्यर्थं रोचयिष्यति ॥ २ ॥

2. Armed with self knowledge thou may'st enjoy
objects (of the world) or engage in action or betake
thyself to meditation, but, O sage, thy mind will ever
be attracted towards That which transcends all objects.

आयासात्सकलो दुःखी नैनं जानाति कश्चन ॥
अनेनैवोपदेशेन धन्यः प्राप्नोति निर्वृतिम् ॥ ३ ॥

3. All exertion causes pain, but no one knows it to
be so. Blessed is he who gets peace from this very lesson.

व्यापारे खिद्यते यस्तु निमेषोन्मेषयोरपि ॥
तस्यालस्यधुरीणस्य सुखं नान्यस्य कस्यचित् ॥४॥

4. He who feels even the motion of his eyelids to
be a burden, even to such a one who is skilled in inaction, is there happiness, to no one else.

are in the realm of the finite and the phenomenal. All that is possible in
the realm of the absolute is negation of the finite. The rest is silence.
Says Vashishtha "May I be this, or may I have this, is the world. The
disappearance of this notion is Moksha. Just as a drop of oil does not cling
to a mirror, but immediately flows down, in the same manner when the
mind has become freed of this notion of "may I be this," the world ceases
to cling to it. It is memory which is the cause of the world. The
suppression of the recollection of both things known and unknown, is supreme felicity. This universal forgetfulness is attained by no other
means but knowledge of Self; when the mind ceases to be mind, i, e.,
function both in and outside itself. When such a stage is reached, then all
bonds are destroyed, "With uplifted arms do I cry," says Vashishtha, but do
no one hears me. Making the mind free of all thought (vacant) is supreme
bliss, why do you not strive for it" It is however not given to every one
to attain to such a condition. This is the sixth stage of knowledge which
if it is attained after many incarnations is considered to be a blessing.
In this stage for the Yogi or Gyani not only the visible, but also all
functions of his own mind cease to exist and like fire without fuel he
attains to Nirvana. This is the universal forgetfulness spoken of in
this section. The whole of the Vedanta Philosophy from the Upanishads
downwards has this object in view and the last word of the Philosophy
is "where one sees not another, hears not another, cognizes not another,
that is Bhumá (infinity) immensity, bliss, immortality. All else is finite,
perishable painful." So conclude the Upanishads.

इदं कृतमिदं नेति द्वंद्वैर्मुक्तं यदा मनः ॥
धर्मार्थकाममोक्षेषु निरपेक्षं तदा भवेत् ॥ ५ ॥

5. "This has been done," "this has not been done," when the mind is free from these conflicting thoughts, it becomes indifferent to virtue, wealth, pleasure and release.

विरक्तो विषयद्वेष्टा रागी विषयलोलुपः ॥
ग्रहमोक्षविहीनस्तु न विरक्तो न रागवान् ॥ ६ ॥

6. The ascetic avoids objects of sense, the man of the world runs after them, but he who is free from both, neither runs after them nor avoids them.

हेयोपादेयता तावत्संसारविटपांकुरः ॥
स्पृहा जीवति यावद्वै निर्विचारदशास्पदम् ॥ ७ ॥

7. So long as desire, the offspring of ignorance is alive, so long there is attachment and aversion, the seed and the sprout of the tree of the Sansára.

प्रवृत्तौ जायते रागो निवृत्तौ द्वेष एव हि ॥
निर्द्वंद्वो बालवद्धीमानेवमेव व्यवस्थितः ॥ ८ ॥

8. Action breeds attachment. Cessation from action leads to aversion. The man of wisdom free from both these opposites is, like a child, above both.

हातुमिच्छति संसारं रागी दुःखजिहासया ॥
वीतरागो हि निर्दुःखस्तस्मिन्नपि न खिद्यति ॥ ९ ॥

9. One attached to the world longs for renunciation to get rid of his trouble. But one without attachment

is free from sorrow, and is not unhappy even by living in the world.

यस्याभिमानो मोक्षेऽपि देहेऽपि ममता तथा ॥
न च ज्ञानी न वा योगी केवलं दुःखभागसौ ॥१०॥

10. One who even in the state of release is as much conscious of it as he is of his body, is neither a Sage nor a Yogi, but is verily destined to be unhappy.

हरो यद्युपदेष्टा ते हरिः कमलजोऽपि वा ॥
तथापि न तव स्वास्थ्यं सर्वविस्मरणाद्दते ॥११॥

11. Let Mahádeva or Vishnu or Brahmá himself be thy preceptor, but there is no peace for thee, except in universal forgetfulness. [1]

CHAPTER 17.

Twenty verses on the condition of the knower of Self.

तेन ज्ञानफलं प्राप्तं योगाभ्यासफलं तथा ॥
तृप्तः स्वच्छेंद्रियो नित्यमेकाकी रमते तु यः ॥१॥

1. Says the Teacher :—He has verily gained the fruit of knowledge, and the fruit of the practice of Yoga, who self-contained, with senses purified, ever remains in seclusion.

न कदाचिज्जगत्यस्मिन् तत्त्वज्ञो हंत खिद्यति ॥
यत एकेन तेनेदं पूर्णं ब्रह्मांडमंडलम् ॥ २ ॥

---

(1) Says Vashishtha. "Taking its stand upon the teaching of the Shastras that nothing here *is*, the mind becomes free from sorrow, and seeing the world as if it were not, it leaves off its vicious character, *i. e.*, is merged into the átmá," a teaching which should be realized to be appreciated.

2. The knower of truth never feels unhappy in this world, because he by his own Self pervades the whole of this universe.

न जातु विषयाः केऽपि स्वारामं हर्षयंत्यमी ॥
सल्लकीपल्लवप्रीतमिवेभं निंबपल्लवाः ॥ ३ ॥

3. These objects of the senses never afford delight to one who finds satisfaction in his own Self. The leaves of the *nim* tree afford no satisfaction to the elephant who loves to feed upon the leaves of the *Salaki* tree.

यस्तु भोगेषु भुक्तेषु न भवत्यधिवासिता ॥
अभुक्तेषु निराकांक्षी तादृशो भवदुर्लभः ॥ ४ ॥

4. One who does not cherish affection for things known, nor runs after those unknown, is a rare in the world.

बुभुक्षुरिह संसारे मुमुक्षुरपि दृश्यते ॥
भोगमोक्षनिराकांक्षी विरलो हि महाशयः ॥ ५ ॥

5. The man of pleasure as well as the aspirant of release are both found in this world. But the great soul who does not care for either, is rare in the world.

धर्मार्थकाममोक्षेषु जीविते मरणे तथा ॥
कस्याप्युदारचित्तस्य हेयोपादेयता न हि ॥ ६ ॥

6. It is only some one of great soul who has neither love nor hatred for Dharma (virtue), wealth (Artha) pleasure (Kám), emancipation (Moksha), life or death.

वांछा न विश्वविलये न द्वेषस्तस्य च स्थितौ ॥

यथा जीविकया तस्माद्धन्य आस्ते यथासुखम् ॥७॥

7. He who feels no anxiety for the cessation of earthly life nor aversion towards its continuance, but takes what comes in the course of things, is happy.

कृतार्थोऽनेन ज्ञानेनेत्येवं गलितधीः कृती ॥

पश्यन् श्रृण्वन् स्पृशन् जिघ्रन्नदन्नास्ते यथासुखम् ॥८॥

8. Having attained his object with the knowledge of Self, with his mind absorbed in it, he lives happy, whether seeing, hearing, touching, smelling or eating.

शून्या दृष्टिर्वृथा चेष्टा विकलानींद्रियाणि च ॥

न स्पृहा न विरक्तिर्वा क्षीणसंसारसागरे ॥ ९ ॥

9. To the person for whom this ocean of world has become dried up, action of the mind becomes objectless, action of the body fruitless and action of the senses automatic. [1]

न जागर्ति न निद्राति नोन्मीलति न मीलति ॥

अहो परदशा कापि वर्त्तते मुक्तचेतसः ॥ १० ॥

---

(1) "Let this be so." "May I have or be this." This thought is the world, (Sansára) and the absence thereof through universal forgetfulness, the place of peace. This is the finále of the Vedanta. Therefore the mind of the knower of Self, even if it acts, does not in reality act. He discharges the functions of the body and senses without being moved by them. He is so to speak oblivious to the world around him. What to others is day, is night to him. He is freed of both attachment and aversion. Renunciation does not consist in cessation of action of the senses or the mind but the absence of attachment thereto. "The great renouncer", says Vashishtha, "is he who has detached himself from and has renounced through the intellect, both Dharma and Adharma, (virtue and vice), pleasure and pain, life and death,—whose desires, and doubts, actions and conclusions are all set at rest, who has ceased to identify himself with the pleasures and pains of the body, and the senses, who knows that he is not the body, nor is this body his."

10. Oh ! wonderful is the condition of the truly liberated soul who is neither awake nor asleep, neither winking nor not winking.

सर्वत्र ह्रयते स्वस्थः सर्वत्र विमलाशयः ॥
समस्तवासनामुक्तो मुक्तः सर्वत्र राजते ॥ ११ ॥

11. At peace everywhere, with a pure heart, free from all desire, he the freed soul, shines everywhere.

पश्यन् श्रृणवन् स्पृशन् जिघ्रन्नदनन्गृह्लन्वदन् व्रजन् ॥
ईहितानीहितैर्मुक्तो मुक्त एव महाशयः ॥ १२ ॥

12. Seeing, hearing, touching, smelling, eating, taking, speaking and moving, the sage is free from both attachment and aversion. The man of great soul is verily free.

न निंदति न च स्तौति न हृष्यति न कुप्यति ॥
न ददाति न गृह्लाति मुक्तः सर्वत्र नीरसः ॥१३॥

13. The man of liberated soul neither blames nor praises, is neither happy nor grieved, neither takes nor gives. He is ever free from attachment.

सानुरागां स्त्रियां दृष्ट्वा मृत्युं वा समुपस्थितम् ॥
अविह्वलमनाः स्वस्थो मुक्त एव महाशयः ॥१४॥

14. At the sight of a woman full of love or on the approach of death, the man of great soul is ever unmoved. He is verily free.

सुखे दुःखे नरे नार्यां संपत्सु च विपत्सु च ॥
विशेषो नैव धीरस्य सर्वत्र समदर्शिनः ॥ १५ ॥

15. Pleasure and pain, man and woman, affluence and poverty make no difference to the sage, who sees unity everywhere.

न हिंसा नैव कारुण्यं नौद्धत्यं न च दीनता ॥
नाश्चर्यं नैव च क्षोभः क्षीणसंसरणेऽनरे ॥ १६ ॥

16. For one to whom the world has ceased to exist, neither is there causing of injury, nor forgiveness, neither pride nor dejection, neither wonder nor perturbation of spirit.

न मुक्तो विषयद्वेष्टा न वा विषयलोलुपः ॥
असंसक्तमना नित्यं प्राप्ताप्राप्तमुपाश्नुते ॥ १७ ॥

17. The released soul neither shuns objects of sense, nor hankers after them, with a mind ever unattached, he takes what comes.

समाधानासमाधानहिताहितविकल्पना ॥
शून्यचित्तो न जानाति कैवल्यमिव संस्थितः ॥१८॥

18. One whose mind has ceased to act, knows neither suppression of the mind nor action thereof, neither its running after the pleasurable, nor avoiding the painful. He abides in unity.

निर्ममो निरहंकारो न किंचिदिति निश्चितः ॥
अंतर्गलितसर्वाशः कुर्वन्नपि करोति न ॥ १९ ॥

19. Free from all sense of "I" or "mine" and realizing that all is nothing, with all desires at rest, though doing he is not doing.

मनःप्रकाशसंमोहस्वप्नजाड्यविवर्जितः ॥
दशां कामपि संप्राप्तो भवेद्गलितमानसः ॥२०॥

20.   He whose mind has become merged in the self (Átmá) is free from specific cognition, dream and dullness. He attains to a condition which is indescribable.[1]

CHAPTER 18.
Hundred verses on Peace.

यस्य बोधोदये तावत्स्वप्नवद्भवति भ्रमः ॥
तस्मै सुखैकरूपाय नमः शांताय तेजसे ॥ १ ॥

1.   Says the Teacher :—Reverence to That upon the rising of the knowledge of which this illusory world becomes a dream, to That whose nature is verily bliss itself, which is ever serene, ever effulgent.

अर्जयित्वाऽखिलानर्थान् भोगानाप्नोति पुष्कलान् ॥
न हि सर्वपरित्यागमंतरेण सुखी भवेत् ॥ २ ॥

2.   One derives pleasure through attainment of worldly objects.   But without universal renunciation he does not become happy.

---

(1) The condition of the knower of Self can only be known to himself or to one like himself, and then also by long companionship.   The question was lately put to a Vedantin and the reply was that knowledge of Brahman is more an object of self realization than capable of being known to others and yet said he, there are some indications of the wise which are unmistakeable.   When all sense of "I" or mine is gone, desire, aversion, passion, pride, delusion, hankering after worldly objects, and causing pain to others in thought and deed, all disappear.   If ever any of these succeeds in asserting its sway, like a line drawn on sand or over the surface of water, it is only asserted to disappear at the next moment. Peace, contentment, cheerfulness, resignation, absence of all thought of Self, humility, and universal love reign supreme, and the sage has a kind word, a kind look, a kind thought and kind action for every body.   The latest case in point is that of Swami Ram Tirtha who has just passed away.   His was a personality never to be forgotten.   An embodiment of unselfish love, ever bright, ever smiling, be inspired love whereever he went.

कर्त्तव्यदुःखमार्तडज्वालादग्धांतरात्मनः ॥
कुतः प्रशमपीयूषधारासारमृते सुखम् ॥ ३ ॥

3. To one whose mind is being scorched by the heat of the sun of things to be done, where is peace except in its being watered by the showers of the ambrosia of contentment?

भवोऽयं भावनामात्रो न किंचित्परमार्थतः ॥
नास्त्यभावः स्वभावानां भावाभावविभाविनाम् ॥४॥

4. The phenomenal is nothing but a state of consciousness. In reality it has no existence. The entities which experience existence and non-existence never cease to be. [1]

न दूरं न च संकोचाल्लब्धमेवात्मनः पदम् ॥
निर्विकल्पं निरायासं निर्विकारं निरंजनम् ॥ ५ ॥

5. Not far off, nor limited, ever present is the Átmá free from all distraction, all sorrow, all change, and all blemish.

व्यामोहमात्रविरतौ स्वरूपादानमात्रतः
वीतशोका विराजंते निरावरणदृष्टयः ॥ ६ ॥

---

(1) The world is but a reflex of the mind, and the only difference between the world of dream and the world of the waking condition, is that in the one the mind acts in what it has created *in* itself; in the other *upon* what it has projected out of itself. The notion of the I, is coexistent with the mind. With the disappearance of the I, the world ceases to exist and what is left is not nothing or vacuity, but pure consciousness which only those who realize it know to be the only reality. Therefore the entity which experiences both existence and non-existence is not the mind but the Self (Átmá) which never ceases to be. In other words—that which connects two states of consciousness is the Átmá or Brahman.

6. Through mere disappearance of illusion, through mere allowment of self, shine those of clear vision with all sorrow gone ! [1]

समस्तं कल्पनामात्रमात्मा मुक्तः सनातनः ॥
इति विज्ञाय धीरो हि किमभ्यस्यति बालवत् ॥७॥

7. All this is merely an action of the mind. The Atmá is ever free, everlasting ; knowing this, will the sage engage in action like a child ?

आत्मा ब्रह्मेति निश्चित्य भावाभावौ च कल्पितौ ॥
निष्कामः किं विजानाति किं ब्रूते च करोति किम् ॥८॥

8. Knowing that his own self is Brahman, and existence and non-existence are due to superimposition alone, what should one who is free from desire, know, say or do ?

अयं सोऽहमयं नाहमिति क्षीणा विकल्पनाः ॥
सर्वमात्मेति निश्चित्य तूष्णींभूतस्य योगिनः ॥९॥

9. "This is I" "This is not I," such notions do not trouble the Yogi who knowing that all is Self, has become silent.

न विक्षेपो न चैकाग्र्यं नातिबोधो न मूढता ॥
न सुखं न च वा दुःखमुपशांतस्य योगिनः ॥१०॥

---

(1) There are three states of the Self, (1) where he identifies himself with and acts in the body, the organs of senses and the mind, (2) where having drawn himself inwards, he acts in a world of his own creation as in a dream, (3) where he abides in his own true self which is beginning-less and endless. The first two are the domain of Avidyá or illusion and should be got rid of by knowledge. The last is that in which one should ever seek to abide. Like a blacksmith cutting a piece of hot iron with cold steel, he should make a mind full of peace and renunciation cut a mind burning with desire.

10. For the Yogi who has found peace, there is no distraction, no concentration, no excess of knowledge, no ignorance, no pleasure, no pain.

स्वाराज्ये भैक्ष्यवृत्तौ च लाभालाभे जने वने ॥
निर्विकल्पस्वभावस्य न विशेषोऽस्ति योगिनः ॥११॥

11. To the Yogi whose mind has ceased to act, ruling a kingdom or going about as a beggar, gain or loss, living in society or in solitude, makes no difference.

क्व धर्मः क्व च वा कामः क्व चार्थः क्व विवेकता ॥
इदं कृतमिदं नेति द्वन्द्वैर्मुक्तस्य योगिनः ॥ १२ ॥

12. Where is virtue, where pleasure, where wealth, where knowledge, where the sense of this has been done, this not, for the Yogi who is free from all sense of duality [1]?

कृत्यं किमपि नैवास्ति न कापि हृदि रंजना ॥
यथा जीवनमेवेह जीवन्मुक्तस्य योगिनः ॥१३॥

13. For the Yogi who is released even in this life, who takes things as they come, there is nothing whatever to do, no yearning for anything whatever.

क्व मोहः क्व च वा विश्वं क्व तच्छ्यानं क्व मुक्तता ॥
सर्वसंकल्पसीमायां विश्रांतस्य महात्मनः ॥१४॥

14. Where is delusion, where the world, where any thought thereof, where release from it for the man of great soul who has found his rest in the goal of all desire (Brahman) ?

_____

(1) Dwanda is really equal to "relativity" as opposed to "unity" or absolute.

येन विश्वमिदं दृष्टं स नास्तीति करोतु वै ॥
निर्वासनः किं कुरुते पश्यन्नपि न पश्यति ॥१५॥

15. One who sees the world may deny its existence. But what does one who has no desire, to do ? Seeing he does not see.

येन दृष्टं परं ब्रह्म सोऽहं ब्रह्मेति चिंतयेत् ॥
किं चिंतयति निश्चितो द्वितीयं यो न पश्यति ॥१६॥

16. He who sees the Supreme Brahman (as separate from himself) may meditate upon " I am Brahman." But what can the Sage who has transcended thought itself meditate upon when he sees no duality ?

दृष्टो येनात्मविक्षेपो निरोधं कुरुते त्वसौ ॥
उदारस्तु न विक्षिप्तः साध्याभावात्करोति किम् १७

17. He who has seen distraction in the Self, may engage in controlling it. The man of the great soul is not distracted. Having nothing to accomplish, what is there for him to do ?

धीरो लोकविपर्यस्तो वर्तमानोऽपि लोकवत् ॥
न समाधिं न विक्षेपं न लेपं स्वस्य पश्यति ॥१८॥

18. The sage though acting like the ordinary man of the world, is yet free from its anxieties. He sees for himself neither concentration of the mind nor its distraction, nor attachment to anything.

भावाभावविहीनो यस्तृप्तो निर्वासनो बुधः ॥
नैव किंचित्कृतं तेन लोकदृष्ट्या विकुर्वता ॥१९॥

7

19. The man of wisdom who is free from all sense of existence and non-existence, who is self satisfied and is free from all desires, does nothing even though he may be acting in the sight of the world.

प्रवृत्तौ वा निवृत्तौ वा नैव धीरस्य दुर्ग्रहः ॥
यदा यत्कर्त्तुमायाति तत्कृत्वा तिष्ठतः सुखम् ॥२०॥

20. For the man of firm intellect there is no anxiety either for action or inaction, he does what comes to him and is ever happy.

निर्वासनो निरालंबः स्वच्छंदो मुक्तबंधनः ॥
क्षिप्तः संस्कारवातेन चेष्टते शुष्कपर्णवत् ॥ २१ ॥

21. Above all attachment and thought of action, free and with all his fetters broken, he moves impelled by the activity of his past *karma*, like a dry leaf impelled by the wind.

असंसारस्य तु कापि न हर्षो न विषादता ॥
स शीतलमना नित्यं विदेह इव राजते ॥ २२ ॥

22. For one who has found his way out of the Sansára, there is no joy, no sorrow ; ever cool and calm, he lives as if he were without a body.

कुत्रापि न जिहासास्ति नाशो वापि न कुत्रचित् ॥
आत्मारामस्य धीरस्य शीतलाच्छतरात्मनः ॥२३॥

23. For one who finds his happiness in his own self, whose mind is calm and pure, there is no desire for renunciation nor any expectation whatever.

प्रकृत्या शून्यचित्तस्य कुर्वतोऽस्य यदृच्छया ॥
प्राकृतस्येव धीरस्य न मानो नावमानता ॥२४॥

24. For one who is self-controlled, whose mind does not act, whose actions are impelled only by past Karma, there is neither honor nor dishonor, even though he may be acting like an ordinary person.

कृतं देहेन कर्मेदं न मया शुद्धरूपिणा ॥
इति चिंतानुरोधी यः कुर्वन्नपि करोति न ॥२५॥

25. He who knows that it is the body which is acting, not he the pure Self, such a one, even though acting, does not in reality act.

अतद्वादीव कुरुते न भवेदपि बालिशः ॥
जीवन्मुक्तः सुखी श्रीमान् संसरन्नपि शोभते ॥२६॥

26. Without saying that he is doing this, the man of released soul does his part in life and is yet not like a child. He moves in the world happy and looks attractive and blessed with good fortune.

नानाविचारसुश्रांतो धीरो विश्रांतिमागतः ॥
न कल्पते न जानाति न श्रृणोति न पश्यति ॥२७॥

27. Wearied of diverse thoughts, the sage has found his peace. He does not desire, nor perceives, nor sees nor hears anything.

असमाधेरविक्षेपान्न मुमुक्षुर्न चेतरः ॥
निश्चित्य कल्पितं पश्यन्ब्रह्मैवास्ते महाशयः ॥२८॥

28. The man of great soul is neither an aspirant of release for he does not long for Samádhi, nor is he bound by the world because for him there is no distraction ; knowing that all is illusion, he abides in his own Self like Brahman himself.

यस्यांतः स्यादहंकारो न करोति करोति सः ॥
निरहंकारधीरेण न किंचिदकृतं कृतम् ॥ २९ ॥

29. He who has the sense of the " I " in him, is acting even though he does not act. But for the sage who is free from all sense of the " I," there is no action, even in action.

नोद्विग्नं न च संतुष्टमकर्तृ स्पंदवर्जितम् ॥
निराशं गतसंदेहं चित्तं मुक्तस्य राजते ॥ ३० ॥

30. The mind of the emancipate is unruffled ; it is neither pleased nor does it act, free from desire and doubt, it shines.

निध्यातुं चेष्टितुं वापि यच्चित्तं न प्रवर्त्तते ॥
निर्निमित्तामिदं किंतु निध्यायति विचेष्टते ॥३१॥

31. The mind which does not hanker either towards rest or motion, engages in action and works as if without a motive.

तत्त्वं यथार्थमाकर्ण्य मंदः प्राप्नोति मूढताम् ॥
अथवायाति संकोचममूढः कोऽपि मूढवत् ॥३२॥

32. One of weak intellect becomes puzzled on hearing truth expounded as it is, or takes to meditation in

order to know the meaning of the Sastras. It is only some one, who though not a child, acts like one. [1]

एकाग्रता निरोधो वा मूढैरभ्यस्यते श्रृशम् ॥
धीराः कृत्यं न पश्यंति सुसवस्त्वपदे स्थिताः ॥३३॥

33. Concentration and subjugation of the mind are the constant refuge of the foolish. The wise do not see anything to be done, they rest in their own self like persons in sleep [2].

अप्रयत्नात्प्रयत्न द्वा मूढो नाप्नोति निर्घृतिम् ॥
तत्त्वनिश्चयमात्रेण प्राज्ञो भवति निर्घृतः ॥ ३४ ॥

34. The fool does not attain to peace either by action or inaction, the sage finds his rest by mere ascertainment of truth.

शुद्धं बुद्धं प्रियं पूर्णं निष्प्रपंचं निरामयम् ॥
आत्मानं तं न जानंति तत्राभ्यासपरा जनाः ॥ ३५ ॥

35. Those in whom the body consciousness is yet powerful on account of past *karma*, do not know the Atmá which is pure intelligence, the object of supreme love, the perfect, above the Sansara and unblemished, and engage in diverse practices towards its attainment.

(1) Brahman as described in the Vedanta does puzzle the ordinary mind, which cannot reconcile itself to statements like these.—" He is beyond the known as well as the unknown. He is beyond speech and thought. He is known to those who do not know him and unknown to those who know him. He guides the senses and is yet above them." But the philosopher knows this to be the only way of describing that which is left after negation of the finite.

(2) On rising from Samadhi the world reasserts itself to one who practises it, not to the knower of the Self in the last stage who sees nothing but the Self everywhere.

नाप्नोति कर्मणा मोक्षं विमूढोऽभ्यासरूपिणा ॥
धन्यो विज्ञानमात्रेण मुक्तस्तिष्ठत्यविक्रियः ॥३६॥

36. The fool does not attain to emancipation even
by constant practice. The blessed one attains to freedom from action by mere knowledge (realization).

मूढो नाप्नोति तद्ब्रह्म यतो भवितुमिच्छति ॥
अनिच्छन्नपि धीरो हि परब्रह्मस्वरूपभाक् ॥३७॥

37. The fool does not attain to Brahman because
he wishes to become it. But the sage is the very Self
of Brahman without wishing for it.

निराधारा ग्रहव्यग्रा मूढाः संसारपोषकाः ॥
एतस्यानर्थमूलस्य मूलच्छेदः कृतो बुधैः ॥३८॥

38. Fools, since they have no firm foundation and
are only anxious to attain Brahman or Mukti, only bind
themselves faster to the world. The wise however cut
off the root of this world, the source of all misery.

न शांतिं लभते मूढो यतः शामितुमिच्छति ॥
धीरस्तत्त्वं विनिश्चित्य सर्वदा शांतमानसः ॥३९॥

39. The fool does not attain to peace because he
strives to attain it. But the Sage having ascertained
truth, has his mind always at peace.

क्वात्मनो दर्शनं तस्य यद्दृष्टमवलंबते ॥
धीरास्तं न पश्यंति पश्यंत्यात्मानमव्ययम् ॥४०॥

40. How can vision of Self be for him who clings

to the visible ? The wise see it not (the phenomenal); they see their own immortal Self.

क्व निरोधो विमूढस्य यो निर्बंधं करोति वै ॥
स्वारामस्यैव धीरस्य सर्वदाऽसावकृत्रिमः ॥४१॥

41. How can Samádhi be for the fool who strives after the breaking of bonds ? Of the sage who finds his happiness in his own Self, the mind is always suppressed without effort.

भावस्य भावकः कश्चिन्न किंचिद्भावकोऽपरः ॥
उभयाभावकः कश्चिदेवमेव निराकुलः ॥४२॥

42. One believes the visible to be in fact existing. Another says that it does not really exist. But it is only some one who knows neither existence nor non-existence and is thus free from distraction.

शुद्धमद्वयमात्मानं भावयंति कुबुद्धयः ॥
न तु जानंति संमोहाद्यावज्जीवमनिर्वृताः ॥४३॥

43. Men of crooked understandings meditate upon the Átmá the ever pure and one without a second, but perceive it not through delusion, and therefore find no peace all their lives.

मुमुक्षोर्बुद्धिरालंबमंतरेण न विद्यते ॥
निरालंबैव निष्कामा बुद्धिर्मुक्तस्य सर्वदा ॥४४॥

44. The intellect of the aspirant for release cannot remain without a support. But the intellect of one who has been released requires no support, and is ever free from desire.

विषयद्वीपिनो वीक्ष्य चकिताः शरणार्थिनः ॥
विशंति झटिति क्रोडं निरोधैकाग्रसिद्धये ॥ ४५ ॥

45. Fools on seeing those tigers known as objects of sense rushing towards them, get frightened and forthwith take refuge in the cave of suppression of the mind and go into meditation or concentration, not so the wise who heed them not.

निर्वासनं हरिं दृष्ट्वा तूष्णीं विषयदंतिनः ॥
पलायंते न शक्तास्ते सेवंते कृतचाटवः ॥ ४६ ॥

46. Elephants of sensual delights on seeing the tiger of renunciation either fly away or like parasites serving a rich person, serve him.

न मुक्तिकारिकां धत्ते निःशंको युक्तमानसः ॥
पश्यन्श्रृण्वन् स्पृशन्जिघ्रन्नश्नास्ते यथासुखम् ॥४७॥

47. The man whose mind ever rests in the Átmá and whose doubts have been removed, does not strive for the means of obtaining release. Seeing, hearing, touching, smelling, eating, he is happy.

वस्तुश्रवणमात्रेण शुद्धबुद्धिर्निराकुलः ॥
नैवाचारमनाचारमौदास्यं वा प्रपश्यति ॥४८॥

48. One whose intellect has become pure and free from distraction by mere listening to (knowledge of) *the thing in itself* (Brahman), sees nought to be done or to be avoided, nor betakes himself to inaction.

यदा यत्कर्तुमायाति तदा तत्कुरुते ऋजुः ॥
शुभं वाप्यशुभं वापि तस्य चेष्टा हि बालवत ४६

49. Whatever comes to him, whether pleasant or
unpleasant, that he does straight. His actions are like
those of a child (free from all thought of self).

स्वातंत्र्यात्सुखमाप्नोति स्वातंत्र्याल्लभते परम् ॥
स्वातंत्र्यान्निर्वृतिं गच्छेत्स्वातंत्र्यात्परमं पदम् ॥५०॥

50. Through freedom one attains to happiness,
through freedom to the Supreme, through freedom to
peace and through freedom to the highest abode.

अकर्तृत्वगभोक्तृत्वं स्वात्मनो मन्यते यदा ॥
तदा क्षीणा भवंत्येव समस्ताश्चित्तवृत्तयः ॥ ५१ ॥

51. As soon as one knows that the Átmá is ever
free from both action and enjoyment of the fruit thereof, all actions of the mind become attenuated.

उच्छृंखलाप्यकृतिका स्थितिर्धीरस्य राजते ॥
न तु सस्पृहचित्तस्य शांतिर्मूढस्य कृत्रिमा ॥५२॥

52. The condition of the wise shines even in its
natural freedom, not so the artificial peace of mind of
the fool with desire lurking in the heart.

विलसंति महाभोगैर्विशंति गिरिगह्वरान् ॥
निरस्तकल्पना धीरा अबद्धा मुक्तबुद्धयः ॥५३॥

53. The wise whose minds are ever free, sometimes
enjoy objects of sense, at other times retire into caves of
mountains. Ever firm, ever liberated, their intellects
are not bound to anything.

श्रोत्रियं देवतां तीर्थमंगनां भूपतिं प्रियम् ॥
दृष्ट्वा संपूज्य धीरस्य न कापि हृदि वासना ॥५४॥

54. No desire of any description ever lurks in the heart of the Sage on seeing and honoring a man of learning, a god, a woman, a king or an object of affection.

भृत्यैः पुत्रैः कलत्रैश्च दौहित्रैश्चापि गोत्रजैः ॥
बिहस्य धिक्कृतो योगी न याति विकृतिं मनाक् ॥५५

55. The Yogi never loses in the least his equanimity of temper, even when ridiculed by his own servants, sons, wives, daughter's sons or other relations.

संतुष्टोऽपि न संतुष्टः खिन्नोऽपि न च खिद्यते ॥
तस्याश्चर्यदशां तां तां तादृश एव जानते ॥५६॥

56. Though pleased he is not pleased, though displeased, he is not displeased. His wonderful condition is known only to one like himself.

कर्तव्यैतेव संसारो न तां पश्यंति सूरयः ॥
शून्याकारा निराकारा निर्विकारा निरामयाः ॥५७॥

57. The world is merely an idea of things to be done. But the wise see it not. They are unattached to form, they are without form, ever free from disturbance and trouble[1].

----

(1) The idea of duty is coexistent with the reality of the phenomenal world. When the nature of the phenomenal is known, there is no longer any idea of duty.

अकुर्वन्नपि संक्षोभादव्ययः सर्वत्र मूढधीः ॥
कुर्वन्नपि तु कृत्यानि कुशलो हि निराकुलः ॥५८॥

58. The fool even though not doing anything is ever distracted and uneasy. The sage, even though doing what is to be done, is ever at ease.

सुखमास्ते सुखं शेते सुखमायाति याति च ॥
सुखं वक्ति सुखं भुंक्ते व्यवहारेऽपि शांतधीः ॥५९॥

59. Complacently he sits, complacently he sleeps, happy he goes about and comes, happy he speaks, happy he eats, even in the world, ever the man of serene mind.

स्वभावाद्यस्य नैवार्तिर्लोकवद्व्यवहारिणः ॥
महाह्रद इवाक्षोभ्यो गतक्लेशः सशोभते ॥ ६० ॥

60. He who does not from his very nature feel troubled when acting like other men (on account of the strength of his knowledge of Self), who remains unagitated like a deep lake and has no sorrow, even *he* is happy.

निवृत्तिरपि मूढस्य प्रवृत्तिरुपजायते ॥
प्रवृत्तिरपि धीरस्य निवृत्तिफलभागिनी ॥ ६१ ॥

61. To the fool cessation from action becomes action, to the sage action yields the same fruit as cessation from action.

परिग्रहेषु वैराग्यं प्रायो मूढस्य दृश्यते ॥
देहे विगलिताशस्य क्व रागः क्व विरागता ॥ ६२ ॥

62. It is the fool who only shows distaste for objects of the world, like house, wife, children, body &c., (without trying to learn the root of the disease) but for one who has lost all sense of I in the body, where is attachment or non-attachment ?

भावनाभावनासक्ता दृष्टिर्मूढस्य सर्वदा ॥

भाव्यभावनया सा तु स्वस्थस्याट्दृष्टिरूपिणी ॥६३॥

63. The mind of the fool is always directed to the entertainment of one thought or the suppression of another[2]. But the vision of the sage, though apparently directed towards the world, is not really so directed, he having destroyed all sense of egoism.

सर्वारंभेषु निष्कामो यश्चरेद्वालवन्मुनिः ॥

न लेपस्तस्य शुद्धस्य क्रियमाणेऽपि कर्मणि ॥६४॥

64. For that pure Muni who moves about like a child unattached to all conditions and who is free from desire, there is no defilement, even though he may be busy in the affairs of the world.

स एव धन्य आत्मज्ञः सर्वभावेषु यः समः ॥

पश्यन्शृण्वन्स्पृशन् जिघ्रन्नश्नन्निस्तर्षमानसः ॥६५॥

65. He is verily the blessed knower of the self, who is the same in all conditions, whether seeing, hearing, touching, smelling, eating. His mind is ever free from desire.

क संसारः क चाभासः क साध्यं क च साधनम् ॥

आकाशस्येव धीरस्य निर्विकल्पस्य सर्वदा ॥६६॥

(2) i. e., existence or non-existence.

66. Where is the world, where delusion, where any object of attainment, where the means, of its attainment, for the sage who, like the limitless Ákása, is free from all action of the mind ?

सजयत्यर्थसंन्यासी पूर्णस्वरसविग्रहः ॥
अकृत्रिमोऽनवच्छिन्ने समाधिर्यस्य वर्तते ॥ ६७ ॥

67. He who from his very nature is merged in that which is limitless, abides in his own true self in all its fullness, and conquers all objects of sense. Even he is victorious.

बहुनात्र किमुक्तेन ज्ञाततत्त्वो महाशयः ॥
भोगमोक्षनिराकांक्षी सदा सर्वत्र नीरसः ॥ ६८ ॥

68. What need is there of saying much, the man of great soul who has known the truth, is unattached to both release as well as enjoyment and is always disinclined to everything.

महदादि जगद्वैतं नाममात्रविजृंभितम् ॥
विहाय शुद्धबोधस्य किं कृत्यमवशिष्यते ॥ ६९ ॥

69. This world of relativity consisting of Mahat (Intellect)[1] and the rest, is nothing but a modification of name. What is left for the sage who has relinquished it and whose knowledge is ever pure, to do ?

भ्रमभूतमिदं सर्वं किंचिन्नास्तीति निश्चयी ।
अलक्ष्यस्फुरणः शुद्धः स्वभावेनैव शाम्यति ॥ ७० ॥

---

(1) This refers to the principles composing the universe. These are *Prakriti* (the unmanifested-condition of matter), the *mahat* (its first manifestation as universal intelligence), the *Ahankara* (Ego-ism), *panchtan matras*, (five causal elements), the 11 organs of sensation and action, the mind and the five elements together with their combinations.

70. All this is a mere illusion, a mere nothing. One who knows this for certain, whose light is that which is beyond all ken, which is ever pure, finds peace as if it were natural to him.

शुद्धस्फुरणरूपस्य दृश्यभावमपश्यतः ॥
क्व विधिः क्व च वैराग्यं क्व त्यागः क्व शमोऽपि वा ॥७१॥

71. For one who is of the nature of pure consciousness, and is not conscious of the visible, where is obligation to perform action, where its abandonment, where non-attachment, where even serenity itself ?

स्फुरतोऽनंतरूपेण प्रकृतिं च न पश्यतः ॥
क्व बंधः क्व च वा मोक्षः क्व हर्षः क्व विषादता ॥७२॥

72. For one who sees himself as the Infinite and does not see the Prakriti (nature) where is bondage, where release, where pleasure, where pain ?

बुद्धिपर्यंतसंसारे मायामात्रं विवर्तते ॥
निर्ममो निरहंकारो निष्कामः शोभते बुधः ॥७३॥

73. In the world which is coexistent with the intellect and is superimposed upon the Átmá by the action of the Máyá, the sage who is free from all sense of I or mine, and who is above desire, alone shines.

अक्षयं गतसंतापमात्मानं पश्यतो मुनेः ॥
क्व विद्या क्व च वा विश्वं क्व देहोऽहंममेति वा ॥७४॥

74. For the Muni who sees his Átmá to be free from destruction and pain, where is knowledge, where the world, where this body and where I or mine ?

निरोधादीनि कर्माणि जहाति जडधीर्यदि ।
मनोरथान्प्रलापांश्च कर्तुमाप्नोत्यतत्क्षणात् ७५

75. The moment the man of weak intellect gives up his practice of concentration of the mind &c., he begins to have diverse thoughts and desires in it.

मंदः श्रुत्वापि तद्वस्तु न जहाति विमूढताम् ॥
निर्विकल्पो बहिर्यत्नादंतर्विषयलालसः ॥ ७६ ॥

76. The fool does not give up his folly even after hearing that which is truth itself. Though suppressing mental action by force, he is internally attached to objects of sense.

ज्ञानाद्दलितकर्मा यो लोकदृष्ट्यापि कर्मकृत् ॥
नाप्नोत्यवसरं कर्तुं वक्तुमेव न किंचन ॥ ७७ ॥

77. He whose Karma has been destroyed by knowledge, even though he may be acting in the sight of men, does not get time to do or speak of anything whatever [1].

क्क तमः क्क प्रकाशो वा हानं क्क च न किंचन ॥
निर्विकारस्य धीरस्य निरातंकस्य सर्वदा ॥ ७८ ॥

78. For the man of wisdom who is free from fault, who is ever fearless, where is darkness, where light, what to renounce, what to gain ?

क्क धैर्यं क्क विवेकित्वं क्क निरातंकतापिवा ॥
अनिर्वाच्यस्वभावस्य निःस्वभावस्य योगिनः ७९

---

(1) So absorbed is he in his own Self.

79. Where is fortitude, where wisdom, where even
fearlessness itself, for the Yogi of indescribable nature
who transcends nature itself.

न स्वर्गो न नरको जीवन्मुक्तिनं चैवहि ॥
बहुनात्र किमुक्तेन योगदृष्ट्या न किंचन ॥ ८० ॥

80. There is no heaven, no hell, not even release in
life (Jiwan mukti). What need is there to say much,
in the view of the Yogi there is here nothing whatever?

नैव प्रार्थयते लाभं नालाभेनानुशोचति ॥
धीरस्य शीतलं चित्तममृतेनैव पूरितम् ॥ ८१ ॥

81. The sage does not hanker after gain, nor grieves
at the non-attainment of what was wished for; his mind
is calm and ever full of the water of life .

न शांतं स्तौति निष्कामो न दुष्टमपि निंदति ॥
समदुःखसुखस्तृसः किंचिल्कृत्यं न पश्यति ॥८२॥

82. The man who is free from desire, does not
praise one who is serene, nor blames him who is addicted
to evil ways ; the same in pleasure and pain, always satisfied, he does not see anything for himself to do.

धीरो न द्वेष्टि संसारमात्मानं न दिदृक्षति ॥
हर्षामर्षविनिर्मुक्तो न मृतो न च जीवति ॥ ८३ ॥

83. The sage feels no aversion for the world nor is
anxious to see his own self ; free from joy and sorrow,
he is neither alive nor dead.[1]

_____

. (1) His condition is indescribable. Though dead in the sight of the
world, he lives in his own self.

निःस्नेहः पुत्रदारादौ निष्कामो विषयेषु च ॥
निश्चितः स्वशरीरेऽपि निराशः शोभते बुधः॥८४॥

84. Free from attachment to sons and spouses, above all desire for objects of the world, as well as all care for his own body, the sage shines.

तुष्टिः सर्वत्र धीरस्य यथापातितवर्तिनः ॥
स्वच्छंदं चरतो देशान्यत्रास्तमितशायिनः ॥ ८५ ॥

85. For the sage who takes what comes to him, who moves about free in the world, sleeping where the sun sets upon his head, there is always happiness.

पततूदेतु वा देहो नास्य चिंता महात्मनः ॥
स्वभावभूमिविश्रांतिविस्मृताशेषसंसृतेः ॥ ८६ ॥

86. Let the body come or go, the sage grieves for it not. He has forgotten everything of the world, having found his rest in his own self.

अकिंचनःकामचारो निर्द्वंद्वश्छिन्नसंशयः ॥
असक्तः सर्वभावेषु केवलो रमते बुधः ॥ ८७ ॥

87. The sage who has nothing to look forward, whose movements are free, who is above all pairs of opposites, whose doubts have all been removed, and who is unattached to any condition whatever, alone moves about happy.

निर्ममः शोभते धीरः समलोष्टाश्मकांचनः ॥
सुभिन्नहृदयग्रंथिर्विनिर्धूतरजस्तमः ॥ ८८ ॥

88. The sage whose sense of "mine" has gone, who is unmoved at the sight of a piece of clay, or stone or gold, the fetters of whose heart have been rent

9.

asunder, whose *rajas* and *tamas* (passion and delusion) have been washed off, shines.

सर्वत्रानवधानस्य न किंचिद्वासनाह्वदि ॥

मुक्तात्मनो वितृप्तस्य तुलना केनजायते ॥८९॥

89 What is there to compare with one who has no attachment to anything, who has no thought in the heart, and whose mind is quite free and is completely peaceful ?

जानन्नपि न जानाति पश्यन्नपि न पश्यति ॥

ब्रुवन्नपि न च ब्रूते कोऽन्यो निर्वासनाद्वते ॥९०॥

90. Knowing he does not know, seeing he does not see, speaking he does not speak, who can be such a one except one who is free from all desires ?

भिक्षुर्वा भूपतिर्वापि यो निष्कामः स शोभते ॥

भावेषु गलिता यस्य शोभनाशोभना मतिः ॥९१॥

91. Be he a king or a beggar, he who is free from desire alone reigns supreme, even he whose inclination towards the good and the bad has been completely subjugated. (¹)

---

(1) " Such amongst kings were Janaka of Mithila, Dilipa the ancestor of Rama, and Mandhata ; amongst Asuras Bali and Prahlada; amongst the gods Agni, Soma, Vayu, Brahma, Vishnu and Mahesha; and amongst, rishis Narada and Vishwamitra. Having attained supreme knowledge some like Bhrigu, Bharadwaja, Vishwamitra and Suka betook themselves to the forest; some continued ruling kingdoms like Janaka, Saryati, Mandhata and Sagar ; some like Brihaspati, Chandra and Surya live in the stellar regions ; some like Agni, Vayu, Yama, Tumbura and Narada, live in the mansions of the gods and some like Bali, Sahotra and Prahlada, in the lower regions. Some live in higher and some in lower orders of creation. All things are everywhere in every condition possible in the Atma, the Self of all. Release is two kinds, embodied and disembodied. Unattachment to objects of affection is *mukti*. The state of oneness (kaivalya) is common to both. The embodied is in life, the disembodied after death. To the man of wisdom who always reflects upon the nature of things, this world becomes easy to move in like passing over the foot print of a cow, for one who does not so reflect, it is difficult to cross like a great ocean". (Yoga Vashistha Upasaman Prakarana Chap. 75).

क स्वाच्छंद्यं क्र संकोचः क्र वा तत्त्वविनिश्चयः ॥
निर्व्याजार्जवभूतस्य चरितार्थस्य योगिनः ॥९२॥

92. Where is freedom, where confinement, where
the ascertainment of truth, for the Yogi who has become the embodiment of unimpeachable sincerity and
who has achieved his object ?

आत्मविश्रांतितृप्तेन निराशेन गतार्तिना ॥
अंतर्यदनुभूयेत तत्कथं कस्य कथ्यते ॥९३॥

93. What language can describe and to whom, can
it describe that which he who has found his satisfaction
in his own self, who is free from all desire, whose
trouble has disappeared, feels inside himself ?

सुप्तोऽपि न सुषुप्तौ च स्वप्नेऽपि शयितो न च ॥
जागरेऽपि न जागर्ति धीरस्तृप्तः पदेपदे ॥९४॥

94. The sage though in sound slumber does not
sleep, though dreaming he does not dream, though
awake he is really not awake. He is happy in every
condition.

ज्ञः सर्चितोऽपि निश्चितः सेंद्रियोऽपि निरिंद्रियः ॥
सुबुद्धिरपि निर्बुद्धिः साहंकारोऽनहंकृतिः ॥९५॥

95. The man of knowledge though thinking, is in
truth not thinking, though cognizing through his organs
of sense he is without organs of sense, though having
an intellect he is not having it, and though possessed
of egoism, he is not in reality so possessed.

न सुखी न च वा दुःखी न विरक्तो न संगवान् ॥

न मुमुक्षुर्न वा मुक्तो न किंचिन्न च किंचन ॥९६॥

96. He is neither happy, nor miserable, neither attached, nor free from attachment, neither an aspirant after release, nor in fact released, neither this thing nor that thing.

विक्षेपेऽपि न विक्षिप्तः समाधौ न समाधिमान् ॥

जाड्येऽपि न जडो धन्यः पांडित्येऽपि न पंडितः ९७

97. He is undistracted in distractions, unmeditating even when meditating, never dull even though appearing to be dull, not learned even though appearing to be learned.

मुक्तो यथास्थितिस्वस्थः कृतकर्तव्यनिर्वृतः ॥

समः सर्वत्र वैतृष्ण्यान्न स्मरत्यकृतं कृतम् ॥९८॥

98. One who is released abides in his own nature and takes what comes to him ; he is free from what has to be done or has been done ; he is unagitated under every condition, and being free from desire, does not remember what he has or has not done.

न प्रीयते वन्द्यमानो निन्द्यमानो न कुप्यति ॥

नैवोद्विजति मरणे जीवने नाभिनंदति ॥ ९९ ॥

99. Worshipped he does not feel delighted, spurned at he does not feel angry, he is not agitated at the thought of death, nor welcomes the prospect of a long life.

न धावति जनाकीर्ण नारण्यमुपशांतधीः ॥
यथातथा यत्रतत्र सम एवावतिष्ठते ॥ १०० ॥

100. The man whose mind has found peace, does
not run towards society nor towards the forest. He
lives happy everywhere and under every condition[1].

CHAPTER 19.

Eight verses on the disciple's rest in his Atma.

तत्त्वविज्ञानसंदंशमादाय हृदयोदरात् ॥
नानाविधपरामर्शशल्योद्धारः कृतो मया ॥१॥

1. Says the disciple :—I have now extracted from
the innermost recess of my heart the thorn of conflicting thoughts with the tongs of the knowledge of Truth.

क धर्मः क च वा कामः क चार्थः क विवेकिता ॥
क द्वैतं क च वाऽद्वैतं स्वमाहिम्नि स्थितस्य मे ॥२॥

2. For me who abide in my own glory, where is
virtue, where pleasure, where greatness, where discern-
ment, where unity or diversity ?

क भूतं क भविष्यद्धा वर्तमानमपि क वा ॥
क देशः क च वा नित्यं स्वमाहिम्नि स्थितस्य मे ॥३॥

---

(1) All these contradictory attributes are mentioned here to
indicate the indescribable condition of the sage. Having relinquished
all thought of objects of senses, free from all action at the mind, he
lives, moves about and sleeps happy. For him who has found rest in
his own self (Atma), either the world is not, Brahman alone is, or the
world is nothing but Brahman. The two do not appear separate but one.
Though appearing to act in the sight of men, he does not in reality act,
because he has lost all sense of " I " or " mine."

t

3. Where is the past, where future, where present, where space, where anything else, for me who eternally abide in my own glory ?

क चात्मा क च वानात्मा क शुभं काशुभं तथा ॥
क चिंता क च वार्चिता स्वमहिम्नि स्थितस्य मे ४

4. Where is self or not self, where good or evil, where care or the absence thereof, for me who abide in my own glory ?

क स्वप्नः क सुषुप्तिवा क च जागरणं तथा ॥
क तुरीयं भयं वापि स्वमहिम्नि स्थितस्य मे ॥५॥

5. Where is dream, where sound slumber, where the waking condition, where the fourth state which is beyond these, where fear, for me who abide in my own glory ?

क दूरं क समीपं वा बाह्यं काभ्यंतरं क वा ॥
क स्थूलं क च वा सूक्ष्मं स्वमहिम्नि स्थितस्य मे ॥६॥

6. Where is far or near, inside or outside, gross or subtle, for me who abide in my own glory ?

क मृत्युर्जीवितं वा क लोकाः कास्य क लौकिकम् ॥
क लयः क समाधिर्वा स्वमहिम्नि स्थितस्य मे ७

7. Where is death or life, the world or its worldliness, where merging of the visible or the concentration of thought, for me who abide in my own glory ?

अलं त्रिवर्गकथया योगस्य कथयाप्यलम् ॥
अलं विज्ञानकथया विश्रांतस्य ममात्मनि ॥८॥

8. Enough therefore of all stories about the three objects of life, (virtue, pleasure and profit), enough of all stories of Yoga or wisdom, for me who have found rest in my own self.

CHAPTER 20.

Fourteen verses on the condition of one who is emancipated in life.

क्व भूतानि क्व देहो वा क्वेंद्रियाणि क्व वा मनः ॥
क्व शून्यं क्व च नैराश्यं मत्स्वरूपे निरंजने ॥१॥

1. Says the disciple :—Where are the elements or the body, where the organs of sense or the mind, where void or fulness, or absence of desire in me who am free from blemish ?

क्व शास्त्रं क्वात्मविज्ञानं क्व वा निर्विषयं मनः ॥
क्व तृप्तिः क्व वितृष्णात्वं गतद्वंद्वस्य मे सदा ॥२॥

2. Where is the Sastra or knowledge of self, or even the mind free from thought of objects, or contentment or absence of desire, for me who have lost all sense of duality ?

क्व विद्या क्व च वाविद्या काहं केदं मम क्व वा ॥
क्व बंधः क्व च वा मोक्षः स्वरूपस्य क्व रूपिता ॥३॥

3. Where is knowledge or ignorance, where I or mine, where this or that, where release or bondage or form, for me the Supreme Intelligence ?

क प्रारब्धानि कर्माणि जीवनमुक्तिरपि क वा ।
क तद्विदेह कैवल्यं निर्वेशेषस्य सर्वदा ॥ ४ ॥

4. Where are karmas which gave the present incarnation and are now bearing fruit, where release in life, where unembodied release, for me who have no attributes?

क कर्ता क च वा भोक्ता निष्क्रियं स्फुरणं क वा ॥
कापरोक्षं फलं वा क निःस्वभावस्य मे सदा ॥५॥

5. Where is the actor, where the enjoyer of fruit of action or the rising of thought of action, where the visible result of knowledge, in me who am free from all conditions what ever?

क लोकः क मुमुक्षुर्वा क योगी ज्ञानवान् क वा ॥
क बद्धः क च वा मुक्तः स्वस्वरूपेऽहमद्वये ॥ ६ ॥

6. Where is the world or one who is desirous of release, where is the Yogi or the man of wisdom or one bound or released, for me who abide in my own nature and am without a second?

क सृष्टिः क च संहारः क साध्ये क च साधनम् ॥
क साधकः क सिद्धिर्वा स्वस्वरूपेऽहमद्वये ॥ ७ ॥

7. Where is creation or dissolution, where is the object to be attained or the means of its attainment, where one who strives for it or attainment of success, for me who abide in my own nature free from all duality?

क प्रमाता प्रमाणं वा क प्रमेयं क च प्रमा ॥
क किंचित्क न किंचिद्धा सर्वदा विमलस्य मे ॥८॥

8. Where is the cognizer, the instrument of cognition, the object of cognition or the conception of such object, where is something or want of something, in me who am ever pure ?

कं विक्षेपः क चैकाग्यं क निर्बोधः क मूढता ॥
क हर्षः क विषादो वा सर्वदा निष्क्रियस्य मे ॥९॥

9. Where is distraction or concentration, knowledge or dullness, pleasure or pain, in me who am ever without action ?

का चैष व्यवहारो वा क च सा परमार्थता ॥
क सुखं क च वा दुःखं निर्विमर्शस्य मे सदा ॥१०॥

10. Where is this business of the world, where that condition of spiritual knowledge, where happiness or misery, in me who am always above thought ?

क माया कच च संसारः क प्रीतिर्विरतिः क वा ॥
क जीवः क च तद्ब्रह्म सर्वदा विमलस्य मे ॥११॥

11. Where is illusion, where the world, where affection or the absence thereof, where the embodied self or that which is known as Brahman, in me the ever pure ?

क प्रवृत्तिर्निवृत्तिर्वा क मुक्तिः क च बंधनम् ॥
कूटस्थनिर्विभागस्य स्वस्थस्य मम सर्वदा ॥१२॥

12. Where is activity or inaction, release or bondage for me who am always unchangeable, ever undivided, ever abiding in my own self ?

कोपदेशः क वा शास्त्रं क शिष्यः क च वा गुरुः ॥
क चास्ति एुरुषार्थो वा निस्पाधेः शिवस्य मे ॥१३॥

13. Where is instruction, or the Sastra, disciple or teacher or any object of search for me, the ever blissful, ever free from all limitation.

क चास्ति क च वा नास्ति कास्ति चैकं क च द्वयम् ॥
बहुनात्र किमुक्तेन किंचिन्नोत्तिष्ठते मम ॥ १४ ॥

14. Where is that which is or which is not, where is one or two. What need is there of saying much, there is nothing which takes its rise in me[1]?

CHAPTER 21.
List of Contents.

दश षट् चोपदेशे स्युः श्लोकाश्च पंचविशतिः ॥
सत्यात्मानुभवोल्लासे उपदेशे चतुर्दश ॥ ६ ॥

---

(1) This is the final stage of Gyāna or self-realization, where the knower of Brahman has become Brahman itself, above thought and free from specific cognition. To him all is Chidākāsa (intelligence unbounded). He is the very Self of knowledge. For him there is no other to see, no other to cognize. It is all one. This was illustrated by Rishi Vashishtha who while exhorting Rama to abide in his own self while discharging his duties in life, to make his waking condition one of dreamless slumber and the condition of dreamless slumber his waking condition, to find his rest in that which remained after the union of the two; i. e., in Brahman, to abide in that which subsisted after the negation of all conditions of both unity and diversity, where the I and the world, both ceased to exist, was asked by Rama as to who that Vashishtha was who was speaking. He replied it by silence and when asked for the reason of the silence, replied, that that was the only answer to Rama's question. "All instruction," said he, " Whether in-duality or non-duality is through speech and thought, both of which from their very nature are conditioned, and when the disciple has reached the stage where true knowledge should be imparted to him, then silence is the only means of imparting it. All that is within the range of thought is not out of the sphere of nescience (Avidya). In the last resort silence is the only way of indicating the supreme self. No preceptor can impart to the disciple more than what he himself is and when Brahman in which he abides, is in fact silence, he can only teach his disciple by silence." This is the negation of all that is time, space and causality, the stage of Nirvikalpa, of Yoga.

ட

1. There are 16 Slokas of instruction, 25 showing the realization by the disciple of his own Atma and fourteen the manner in which the Guru questions his pupil's realization of self.

षटुछासे लये चैवोपदेशे च चतुश्रुतुः ॥
पंचकं स्यादनुभवे बंधमोक्षे चतुष्ककम् ॥ २ ॥

2. There are six Slokas showing the bliss of realization, four conveying the method of self-absorption, four showing the manner in which the Atma is known by the wise, and five wherein the disciple re-echoes his knowledge thereof.

निर्वेदोपशमे ज्ञाने एवमेवाष्टकं भवेत् ॥
यथासुखे सप्तकं च शांतौ स्याद्देदसंमितम् ॥ ३ ॥

3. Four treat of release and bondage, eight deal with non attachment and eight treat of the subject of peace, eight with that of knowledge, eight with the true condition of the knower; seven deal with Yathá Sukha (happiness), and four with bliss.

तत्त्वोपदेशे विंशच्च दश ज्ञानोपदेशके ॥
तत्त्वस्वरूपे विंशच्च शमे च शतकं भवेत् ॥ ४ ॥

4. There are 20 Slokas in the instruction about truth, ten in that of knowledge, 20 relate to the nature of truth and 100 to contentment or quietude.

अष्टकं चात्मविश्रांतौ जीवन्मुक्तौ चतुर्दश ।
षट् संख्याक्रमाविज्ञाने ग्रंथकाल्म्य ततः परम् ॥५॥

5. There are 8 *slokas* about rest in the Átmá, 14 about Jiwan mukti and six show the number of verses in the book, after which is a summary of the chapters of the work and of the whole.

विंशत्येकमितैः खंडैः श्लोकैरात्माग्निमध्यखैः ॥
अवधूतानुभूतेश्व श्लोकाः संख्याक्रमा अमी ॥६॥

6. There are 21 sections and 302 verses in the book. The last 303 does not count. The three are the five, (elements), the two are the embodied and supreme Self, and the zero is the Akasa or ether.

ॐ तत्सत् ।

l

CPSIA information can be obtained
at www.ICGtesting.com
Printed in the USA
LVHW03s0225060718
582898LV00013B/477/P

9 781293 678091